TROUBLEMAKERS IN THE CHURCH

"I've listened to Mark tell these stories for over ten years. Some of them make you smile and maybe even laugh. Some make you angry, and some will even make you want to cry. All of them break your heart because they happen in the very place God established to bring healing and hope to people, the church. It is much better to learn from Mark's experiences with these troublemakers than to learn on your own. This book will save you a lot of heartache and pain by giving you the tools and insights on how to better handle the troublemakers you will inevitably face."

—Mike Black, Lead Pastor
Poinciana Christian Church, Kissimmee, Florida

"Mark Atteberry has made real the old adage: 'What makes the church great? People! What makes the church awful? People!' Anyone serving in ministry should read this book. Anyone who has been wounded in church should read this book. It's imperative to know what to say to troublemakers, and to know when and how to say it."

—Greg Bondurant, Lead Minister
Westerville Christian Church, Westerville, Ohio

"In this well-written and extremely practical book, Mark Atteberry says the quiet parts out loud. And as a pastor, I'm so grateful! Every pastor I know wants to quit about once a year. Surprised? Read this book and you'll understand why (and why church members want to quit, too). But more importantly, you'll be better equipped to support your pastor, encourage faithful fellowship within your church family, and recognize troublemakers, even if there's one looking back at you in your own mirror!"

—Arron Chambers, Pastor
Author of *Eats with Sinners: Loving Like Jesus*

"I love the approach of not only identifying the problems but giving solutions. Every leader in every church would benefit from this book. The final chapter alone would save many churches from these types of people."

—Gary Cox, Pastor
First Christian Church, Ft. Myers, Florida

"*Troublemakers in the Church* is a survival manual for ministry, and Mark is a wise and trusted guide. With insight, wisdom, and humor, Mark shares decades of experiences with challenging people and guides us to healthy and God-honoring ways to respond. This book is ministry gold, and it's such a gift for church leaders and everyone who has a heart for ministry. I highly recommend it!"

—Scott Eynon, Lead Pastor
Community Christian Church of Ft. Lauderdale

"Mark's book is on point, honest, and real for anyone who has been a significant part of a church, whether as a pastor, member, or attender. He encourages us all to look inside ourselves to see if we are a part of the problem or the solution."

—Dan Hargrave, Lead Pastor
Stokelan Drive Christian Church, Malden, Missouri

"Fascinating and informative. Mark pinpoints many problems and conflicts that will inevitably occur in the typical church. This book is important, especially for those serving in church leadership positions."

—Kenneth W. Johnson, Church Elder
Professor Emeritus, Lindenwood University

"This book should be required reading for every pastor entering the ministry."

—Brian Jones, Senior Pastor
Christ's Church of the Valley, Philadelphia

"Every Christian should read this book from cover to cover. Some of us need it because of the biblical advice, which is always sage and practical. Others of us need to see the damage we are doing to the body of Christ so we can repent. Thank you for the mirror, Mark!"

—Charlie McGee, Senior Pastor
CrossPoint Christian Church, Mascoutah, Illinois

"It's uncanny the way Mark can humorously size up the people a minister encounters in the local church. Other than the Bible, I believe no other book is as essential to the young minister navigating ministry. It's an invaluable resource."

—Ross Pepper, Retired Pastor

"Somebody once said that hurt people hurt people. We certainly see that in the church. In *Troublemakers in the Church*, Mark Atteberry identifies the different types of people who hurt people and then gives practical steps on how to deal with them. If you're leading, serving, or attending a church, Mark's book is a must-read."

—Steve Poe, Senior Pastor, Northview Church
Author of *Creatures of Habit*

"This book should be required reading for ministers, church members, and ministry students. Like Mark's other books, it's loaded with strong biblical exposition, practical application, humor, and on-target answers to the questions people struggle with."

—Guthrie Veech, Lead Pastor
New Hope Christian Church, Nokomis, Florida

TROUBLEMAKERS IN THE CHURCH

DEALING WITH THE DIFFICULT, THE DANGEROUS, AND THE DEADLY

MARK ATTEBERRY

HENDRICKSON PUBLISHERS
an imprint of Hendrickson Publishing Group

Troublemakers in the Church: Dealing with the Difficult, the Dangerous, and the Deadly

Published by Hendrickson Publishers
an imprint of Hendrickson Publishing Group
Hendrickson Publishers, LLC
P. O. Box 3473
Peabody, Massachusetts 01961-3473
www.hendricksonpublishinggroup.com

ISBN 978-1-4964-7155-0

Printed in the United States of America

First Printing — May 2022

Library of Congress Control Number: 2021953223

For Marilyn

CONTENTS

ACKNOWLEDGMENTS

This book had been inside me, clawing and trying to get out for a few years. In a sense, it was COVID that finally set it free. When our church shut down and I suddenly had more time on my hands, I decided it was time to start writing. No, I am not thanking the virus, just giving you some perspective. Good things can come out of bad situations.

I want to thank the five churches I served during my forty-six years in ministry. In all of them, there were people who loved me, helped me, taught me, encouraged me, endured my weak moments, and forgave my mistakes. They know who they are. I want them all to know I am deeply grateful and feel honored to have served them.

In those churches, there were also people whose stories are told in this book. I am thankful for them as well. In some ways, they taught me more than anybody. Although it wasn't as much fun, the truths I learned benefitted me, and, through this book, I hope they benefit others.

I also want to thank my wife, Marilyn. She walked with me through all forty-six years of my ministry. She knows all the stories in this book because she lived them too. I may have been the one in the trenches, but she was at home, always ready with a listening ear, encouragement, wise counsel, and love. I can't imagine surviving so long in ministry without her.

My agent, Greg Johnson of WordServe Literary, is an awesome guy, a good friend, and a faithful advocate of my work. I am grateful and blessed to be in his stable of authors.

I also want to thank Hendrickson Publishers and especially my editor, Patricia Anders, as well as Sarah Welch. It's wonderful when you write a book and your editor "gets" it. That doesn't always happen, but it did in this case. You can be sure that the version of this book you're reading is far better than the one I first submitted. I'm not sure, but I think Patricia might have superpowers.

Finally, I know that without you, the reader, there would be no point to anything I write. Thank you for supporting my work.

The first mention of Satan's work in the book of Acts occurs not in the Sanhedrin. Nor in the Temple. Nor in Rome. But in the church. It was in church that Peter rebuked Ananias: "Why has Satan filled your heart to lie to the Holy Spirit, and to keep back some of the price of the land?"[1]

—Steven J. Lawson, *Faith under Fire*

INTRODUCTION

The Church: More Dangerous Than You Think

I am a recent trooper from the battlefield of bloody confrontation who tried to be pastoral, loving, understanding, reconciling, and redemptive yet ended up being shot down and left to die on the battlefield of the church, and there are thousands just like me.[2]

Guy Greenfield, *The Wounded Minister*

When I landed my first book deal, my publisher flew me to Nashville and put me through a two-day media training course along with seven other first-time authors. They wanted to make sure that when we started doing interviews, we would have at least some vague idea of how not to embarrass ourselves. Or them.

When I arrived at the seminar, I sat down beside a young man who would go on to become a mega-bestselling author. If I told you his name, I have no doubt you would recognize it. But at that time, he was like me: as green as the turf at Augusta National. We hit it off immediately and ended up hanging out together between sessions. We had long talks about life and faith that were rich and meaningful. To this day, I have mountains of respect for him.

But there was one thing we didn't see eye-to-eye on. When I asked him what church he attended, he said he didn't attend any church. "No offense," he said. "I know you're a pastor, but I'm not a church guy." I was surprised and curious (considering he had just written a Christian book), so I asked him why he wasn't a fan of the church. He answered, "Because the church has let me down too many times." He then shared a few stories that, I have to admit, did not reflect well on the body of Christ. He concluded by saying, "Jesus has never let me down, so I just stick with him and stay away from the church."

I suspect there are millions of people—yes, *millions*—who feel the same way. There was a time in their lives when the church meant a great deal to them; but after repeated hurts and disappointments, they just decided to chuck it and walk away. During my forty-six years as a pastor, I've met a lot of these people. Many of them sincerely love God and were respectful toward me as a pastor, but they wanted nothing to do with the church. I recall one man saying, "I was treated worse by my church than I ever have been treated by the secular company I work for. The church is a lot more dangerous place than people think."

I believe most people would agree that "the church" is an amazing concept—the idea that people who share faith in Christ can worship and serve together and enjoy sweet fellowship that has love, forgiveness, and mutual support as its hallmarks. But the reality is often far different. When people who are a part of the church behave in ways that are thoughtless, selfish, and even vicious, that shining ideal drastically dims and people are wounded. Sometimes they never recover. The one place in the community that should symbolize hope and light can become a house of horrors with blood on the pews.

Why does this happen?

The quick and easy response is to point an accusing finger at Satan and quote Ephesians 6:12: "For we are not fighting against flesh-and-blood enemies, but against evil rulers and authorities of the unseen world, against mighty powers in this dark world, and against evil spirits in the heavenly places." While it's true that we are in a spiritual war that has deep implications for every area of our lives, I fear that a verse like this can become a convenient diversion for us—a way to direct attention away from our own culpability. We're like the guy who runs up credit card debt buying worthless trinkets and then complains about how he can't get ahead financially because the government keeps raising taxes. Sometimes what we need most is a mirror.

I intend for this book to be that mirror.

No, I'm not denying the role Satan plays in church problems. But there have been plenty of books written about that. The problem I see that hasn't been given enough attention is the behavior of people who are supposed to know better: people who walk into the church building every Sunday morning toting the word of God under their arms, smiling, shaking hands, and hugging like politicians running for office, only to then turn around and cause trouble; driving their pastor crazy, becoming undependable, criticizing, gossiping, and much more.

In the pages to come, you'll find a Top 25 list of the most troublesome people in the church, chosen and ranked by me, from least damaging (#25) to most damaging (#1). Each one has an assigned nickname that describes what they do. I'll then cite some examples, offer a few words of insight into each one, and explain how they harm the body of Christ. And I will pull no punches. As someone who has dealt with problem people in the church for almost half a century, someone who has seen blood on the pews—some of it my own—I have long understood that mollycoddling and making excuses for troublesome people accomplishes nothing. I'll warn you now that as we work our way toward #1, the chapters will grow longer and darker.

In Part One, we start with those who are "difficult": people who are relatively harmless (most of the time) but sure do get on your nerves. They've basically turned being frustrating into an art form. In Part Two, we look at the "dangerous": people who aren't killers but have the potential to cause serious trouble. Finally, in Part Three, we deal with the "deadly": people who absolutely *are* killers, and the main reason why there is blood on the pews in so many churches.

I acknowledge that I am not a psychologist or a licensed mental health expert. The opinions I offer about the different types of people in this book are just that: opinions. And they should be taken as such. But they are not the opinions of someone who spent the war in a cushy office far behind the front lines. I spent my life where the bullets were flying and the bombs were being dropped. The people you will read about here are people I've observed, talked to, contended with, tried to help, and often cleaned up after. A Danish proverb says, "He knows the water best who has waded through it."

But this book is more than just a roster of church troublemakers. In Part Four, I will offer a practical, biblical plan for how to protect your church from the troublesome people in this book and create a culture that keeps their influence to a minimum. No church will ever be completely free of difficult people as long as we unlock our doors on Sunday morning and invite people in. But there's plenty you can do keep your church strong and healthy and peaceful.

Before we dig in, I want to talk briefly about why this topic is so rarely addressed. Everybody knows that churches of all kinds are plagued by troublesome people. Most of us, at some point in our lives, have attended a church where such people run amok. But I discovered while researching this book that precious little has been written about the problem. I wonder if at least part of the reason is because of the risk of seeming negative. Perhaps authors don't want to be seen as beating up on the bride of Christ or arrogantly chastising fellow church members.

I look at it differently. In Matthew 7:5, Jesus told us to get the plank out of our own eye before we criticize others. This book certainly meshes with the spirit of that command. Further, Jesus and the apostles warned us that not every threat would come from outside the church. Both Paul's epistles and Jesus' "letters" to the seven churches in Revelation contain dramatic exhortations to do some serious housecleaning. Finally, I contend that self-correction, though painful, is not negative. It's all part of contending for the faith, which is the most positive endeavor in which we will ever engage. As J. C. Ryle said a hundred and fifty years ago, echoing the words of the apostle Paul, "Let us settle in our minds that the Christian fight is a good fight—really good, truly good, emphatically good."[3]

If you're leading, serving, or attending a church that has troublemakers, I pray that this book might inspire you to take a look in the mirror and, if you see a problem, to then take bold action and chart a new course for yourself and your church. If there's going to be blood in our churches, let it be only the blood of Christ, which takes away our sins.

NOTE FROM THE AUTHOR

In an old *Peanuts* comic strip, Lucy is talking to Linus, who has just expressed his desire to be a doctor someday. She says, "You, a doctor. Ha! That's a big laugh. You could never be a doctor. You know why? Because you don't love mankind, that's why."

As she walks away, Linus says, "I love mankind. It's people I can't stand."[4]

Isn't this the challenge we all face?

When God tells us to love our fellow man, we smile sweetly and say, "Yes, Lord." But when he starts naming names, we go into a choking fit. "Surely, Lord, you don't mean I have to love my cheating, deadbeat ex who can always find money to wine and dine his new girlfriend, but never has a dollar to his name when it's time to pay his child support!"

Wouldn't life be *so* much easier if we could just keep things nice and vague?

I bring this up because you are holding in your hands a book that is as far from vague as you can get. As you turn the coming pages, you're going to read about specific types of people that have frustrated you, annoyed you, complicated your life, or possibly caused you deep pain. As you read, the faces of real people you have tangled with will likely flash through your mind. Your blood pressure could shoot up. You might even break out in a cold sweat. I know this because all of these things happened to me as I was writing.

Before that can happen, here's what I recommend you do first:

1. *Pray your way through this book.* If you have a flashback or feel some buried resentment start to awaken in your heart, stop right then and talk to God about it.
2. *Embrace your limitations.* You can't fix these people. Nor will you ever fully understand why they are the way they are. The good news is that God doesn't ask you to.
3. *Keep things in perspective.* Many of the people on this list, while troublesome at times, have good qualities too. Don't fall into the common trap of calling someone a "complete idiot" or a "loser" just because he or she is a challenge.
4. *Remember that you're not perfect either.* Never lose sight of the fact that someone, somewhere, could be reading this book and seeing your face flash before their eyes!
5. Finally, *embrace your calling as a Christian.* Love and pray for those who make your life difficult (Matt. 5:44).

As I've already said, this book pulls no punches. At the same time, it also won't mock, ridicule, or in any way diminish the value of these people's souls. They may be troublesome, but God loves them and so must we.

Consider Moses, whom God put in charge of a few hundred thousand whiners. If anyone was ever qualified to write a book about troublesome people, he was. The Israelites were so bad that even God called them "stubborn and rebellious" and made up his mind to wipe them out and start over (Exod. 32:9–10). Most people in Moses' position would have said, "That's a great idea!" But Moses didn't. Instead, he pleaded with God to change his mind and let the people live (Exod. 32:11–13). It's one of the most striking examples in the entire Bible of what it means to love troublesome people, and it shines a light on our path forward. May we never forget that the world will know we are Christians not by the indignities we've suffered or the scars we bear or the dramatic nature of our war stories, but by the love we have for one another (John 13:35).

A book like this, however, wouldn't work without stories. To just write about negative personality traits and moral weaknesses without showing how they play out in real life would be pointless. This is why coaches use game film. They know their players need more than just hearing about what went wrong; they need to see it.

So I have included lots of stories, most of them short and to the point. You should know that they are true stories that have been fictionalized. That means I have changed certain nonessential details to obscure the identities of those involved. In some cases, I have made men women and women men. In others, I have altered time frames and settings. Be assured, however, that every one of these incidents really happened.

One day shortly before I retired, I told a couple of my coworkers that I honestly thought I had seen everything the ministry could throw at a pastor. "I just can't imagine that there's something that can happen in a church that I haven't seen at least once," I said. The following Sunday, an elderly gentleman walked into our auditorium and stopped in the back to survey the room and find a seat. I was standing about ten feet behind him when, suddenly, his pants fell down and pooled around his ankles. A younger man standing nearby rushed over and helped him pull them back up. The following day at our staff meeting, I told our team that I would never again say I had seen it all. I hope these stories, collected over forty-six years of pastoring, are helpful to you as you deal with the troublemakers in your church one way or another.

PART ONE

THE DIFFICULT

Difficult people make up only a fraction of our daily contacts but cause most of our frustration. . . . They've been called "crazy-makers," "odd ducks," and many less printable names.[5]

Arthur H. Bell and Dayle M. Smith, *Difficult People at Work*

#25

THE NOSTALGIST

Right off the bat, let's give this person some props for being the least troublesome of all the people on this list. I mean, aren't you doing pretty well if there are twenty-four types of people who cause more headaches than you? On the other hand, maybe it's like being #10 on Mr. Blackwell's list of the ten worst-dressed women. There may be nine others who dress worse than you do, but it's still a list you don't want to be on.

At any rate, the nostalgist is a person who clings to the past because, in his or her mind, it holds charms the present does not. To be fair, we all have fond memories we love to talk about. I, for example, love to reminisce about the days when our church dominated our city's parks and recreation softball leagues. Over ten years, we won over forty first- or second-place trophies. Get me started and I can tell stories for hours. But reminiscing about the past is different from clinging to it. You know a person is clinging to the past when he brings it up in every conversation.

- When the subject of music comes up, the nostalgist laments how we don't sing hymns anymore.
- When attendance increases, the nostalgist recalls how nice it was when the congregation was smaller and everybody knew one another.
- When attendance drops, the nostalgist reminds everybody of the time when they had to put folding chairs out to accommodate all the people.

- When the youth group is mentioned, the nostalgist comments on how young people used to be so much more respectful.
- When a new program is announced, the nostalgist explains how the church he used to attend did it differently and, of course, much better.
- And when the preacher describes an exciting vision for the future, the nostalgist speaks of how sad it is that the church is "abandoning the values and principles that got us here."

The nostalgist is not a bad person, but he has a knack for ruining the moment. Instead of just being positive and supportive of what's happening, he always has to diminish it by mentioning a time when things were better. If there's wind in somebody's sails, you can count on the nostalgist to suck it out.

Perhaps the most discouraging thing about the nostalgist is that he is often wrong in his assessment of the past. I was at my last pastorate for thirty-one years, so I had a broad understanding of the history of that church. I saw most of it with my own eyes. I lived it. So when the nostalgists in our church started pontificating about the past, I knew whether they were right or wrong, and most of the time they were wrong! They exaggerated. Sometimes they flat out got their facts wrong, but always in a way to diminish the present in favor of the past.

For years, psychologists have been trying to figure out why people do this. Why does the past seem so much better than it probably was? There are all kinds of theories. One I read about has to do with our subconscious need to keep up our self-image. In order to do this, we have to inhibit negative memories and elevate positive ones.[6] Another study done by Carnegie-Mellon University suggests that it's as simple as people hanging onto what they like and mentally letting go of what they don't like. These researchers compare it to a record store that stocks only the hits of the past, but both the hits and duds of the present.[7] Naturally, the past is going to seem better than it actually was.

Whatever the reason for the nostalgist's love affair with the past, he or she is eventually going to get under the skin of church leaders trying to follow the apostle Paul's example in Philippians 3:13 of forgetting what lies behind and pressing on to what lies ahead. I know all too well that when someone is constantly talking about how great things used to be compared to how they are now, it grates on your nerves. Eventually, you start wondering if the person has any appreciation at all for what you're trying to accomplish. Do they understand the logic behind the changes you're making? You explained it, but were they listening? Do they even care?

Nostalgists are even more frustrating when they jump to immediate conclusions and make grand pronouncements without giving new ideas a chance. Some church members—bless their hearts—are at least open-minded and thoughtful enough to keep their skepticism to themselves until the idea has had a chance to sink or swim. But many start crowing the moment they hear about the change. I recall one lady who, on hearing about a change we were planning, said to me, "I don't recognize this place anymore. Whatever happened to my little church that I fell in love with?"

Here's the good news: Looking back over the two-thousand-plus-year history of the church, nostalgists, for all their pining over the past, have not been able to hold back the church. In New Testament times, the Judaizers clung to the customs and practices of the law of Moses, trying their best not to let them slip away, but the church marched on. In the 1970s, lovers of the King James Version bemoaned "dangerous" new translations of the Bible, but the church marched on. In the 1990s, lovers of traditional hymns clutched their pearls and spoke of how offended they were by the presence of drums and guitars in the sanctuary, but the church marched on.

And so we come to the secret of dealing with a nostalgist: march on.

- When they tell you how their old church used to do it better, march on.
- When they whine about the vision you're casting, march on.
- When they post their frustrations on social media, march on.
- When they tell you they might have to rethink their giving because they're unhappy with the direction of the church, march on.
- When they tell you they're thinking about finding a new church because of the changes you're making, march on.

Don't be smug or condescending, just march on. People will make their choice as to whether they want to march with you or not. Some will and some won't. Even Jesus had people who jumped off the bandwagon (see John 6:66). Your job is to do what's best for the church—and that means marching on.

#24

THE CHURCH HOPPER

There are two kinds of church hoppers.

One is that person (or couple or family) who hops from church to church every couple of years. They come through the door all smiles, telling you what wonderful things they've heard about your church and how happy they are to have found you. They reek of positivity and seem eager to plug right in and serve. But a couple of years later, they're gone. Something about your church wasn't meeting their needs, just like the church they attended before yours wasn't meeting their needs, and the church they attended before that didn't meet their needs. It's not uncommon for people like this to attend and eventually leave every church in the town where they live, and then start working their way through the churches in the towns next door.

One day, a man and his wife visited our church for the first time. On Monday, a pastor friend from a church eight miles away called me and asked if they had showed up at our services that Sunday. When I said yes, he chuckled. "What's so funny?" I asked, even though I was pretty sure I knew what he was going to say. "It's your turn, old buddy," he replied. "They've been members of every church in town and found a fatal flaw in all of them. When they start to feel unhappy, they complain for a while, and then they decide they just can't live with such a gross lack of spirituality and move on. Looks like you guys are next." Sure enough, it took them less than two years to decide we weren't spiritual enough for them.

But there's another kind of church hopper that is just as frustrating. It's that person who never settles into one church but constantly hops from one congregation to another, sometimes within the same week. He might like the music at one church, the preaching at another church, and playing softball with some buddies at a third church. So he splits his time between all three churches. I've even known people who routinely attended two different churches on the same day. They slip into one church to enjoy the terrific worship team, and then slip quietly out the back door and hustle over to another church just in time to hear a preacher they especially enjoy.

I wrote extensively about this in my book *The 10 Dumbest Things Christians Do*.[8] When that book came out, I was invited to appear on a Christian television talk show. The woman who interviewed me was apparently a church hopper of the second type and was ready to pounce. "Mark, I don't understand what's wrong with me attending two or three or even four different churches if I get something I need from each one of them. Why is that a bad thing?" I asked her to think about what would happen if every Christian took that approach. What if none of us committed to a single church but just floated from one to another according to our moods? Would we even *have* any strong churches to float to? I believe the answer to that question is no, we wouldn't, because great churches are not, never have been, and never will be built by church hoppers. They are built by conscientious, hard-working Christians who settle in and knuckle down and do the hard work of ministry week after week, month after month, and year after year. I didn't say this on the air, but that TV host should be thankful from the bottom of her heart for her brothers and sisters in Christ who are *not* church hoppers, for those who have been faithful to their congregations over the long haul and have worked hard for years to build the ministries that were a blessing to her.

When I was young and naive, I thought church hoppers would land in our church and find the cure for their church hopping. I told myself that they would be so well treated that they would learn to love us and wouldn't want to leave. It didn't take too many years for me to realize what a silly pipe dream that was. Regardless of what they say, church hoppers don't hop because the churches they attend are flawed. They hop because something is amiss in their own hearts or thinking.

I'll admit I'm speculating, but it's speculation based on years of experience and observation. Church hoppers, especially the second variety, seem to enjoy being accountable to no one. The Bible clearly teaches that Christians should be submissive and accountable to church leaders (Heb. 13:17), but when you never settle down in one church—when you float in and out the door and never stay put in one place—you avoid having to answer to anyone in authority. You could, for example, be living with obvious immorality in your life. If you were committed to a single church, you would likely be approached about it. But by avoiding commitment to any church, you can stay just out of the range of the church leaders' jurisdiction and never be called to account for your actions.

The bigger issue with church hoppers seems to be their belief that any church that doesn't perfectly meet their needs (or completely measure up to their expectations) is not worthy of their full commitment. Boy, I'm glad my wife didn't think that way when the notion of marrying me was presented to her. She could easily have listed my imperfections and said, "Sorry, I can do better. Bye-bye!" There were many smarter, richer, better-looking guys she could have married. But she understood that there are many more important issues to consider than IQ, money, and looks. She saw my good points and felt I was worthy of her full commitment.

An imperfect church is worthy of a full commitment too. So what if the facilities aren't state of the art? So what if the preacher is a little long-winded? So what if the woman who runs the nursery is uncomfortably outspoken? So what if they sing too many hymns, or not enough? By hopping to another church, you will just swap one set of imperfections for another. It's pointless, really. Unless your church is preaching false doctrine or is engaged in some sort of internal civil war, you are likely better off staying put.

So what's the best way to handle church hoppers?

1. *Don't be naive.* Don't assume yours is going to be the church that cures them. Understand that it's really not about you; it's about them. This will soften the blow when they pack up and leave.
2. *Don't get caught up in trying to make over your church to suit them.* They will eventually come in with complaints and suggestions. Countless pastors (including me) will confess to making changes in an effort to placate people, only to watch them leave anyway.
3. *Don't chase them when they do leave.* Don't try to talk them into coming back. That's another mistake I made when I was young, and it never worked out well. Even when they did come back to "give it another try," they always left again. I eventually learned that our church was much happier and healthier when the only people who were there were those who wanted to be there.

#23

THE NITPICKER

I was twenty-two years old when I accepted the call to my first full-time ministry. Believe me when I tell you that I was *not* full of myself as many young pastors can be. I had just gotten fired from my previous part-time ministry and was wondering if I had what it took to make it as a pastor. I wanted to believe I did, but I knew the next year or two would tell the tale. All I had when I rolled into that town was a wife, a brand-new baby, a few meager possessions, and a whole lot of uncertainty.

It was in that church that I met my first nitpicker. Like quite a few of the people on this list, he was a good person who loved the Lord. I really don't think he meant to drive me crazy. I truly believe he thought he was helping me. In fact, he *did* help me. But he just about broke my spirit in the process.

It was maybe the third or fourth week of my ministry when he asked if he could speak with me in private. Never in a million years would I have guessed what he was going to say. He told me that my sermons were good, but they would be better if my command of the English language improved. Therefore, he said, he would begin taking notes on my sermons the following Sunday. Not for content, mind you, but for grammatical errors and word choices that could be improved. After each service, he would hand me his notes, and I could go over them and try to do better the next week.

Two things bothered me about this. One was that he didn't ask if it was okay with me for him to do this; he straight up informed me that he *was* going to do it. The other thing that bothered me was that he seemed to see me more as one of his students than his pastor. To him, my sermons were papers that needed to be graded rather than messages from the Bible that needed to be taken to heart. But I was twenty-two, desperate to get off to a good start, and terrified of making some influential person mad right out of the gate, so I kept my mouth shut.

Sure enough, for the next several months, I was handed a sheet of paper after every Sunday morning service that listed all my mistakes. It was a ritual I came to loathe—not because I doubted the legitimacy of his criticisms, but because of the general negativity of the whole exercise. What person in any profession would like to be handed a list of all his mistakes at the end of every workday?

- *Sorry, you used "who" when you should have used "whom."*
- *Oops, you ended that sentence with a preposition.*
- *You simply must learn the difference between "If I was" and "If I were."*

But this is what nitpickers do. They find errors, slip-ups, and miscues like metal detectors find bottle caps. What's worse, they're happy about it. They're like kids finding Easter eggs. Ask any church administrator who prints the bulletin. She will tell you that there's no glee like the glee of a church member who finds a typo. That person will practically climb over the pews to get to her and tell her.

A person who nitpicks may have one or more of several issues. He may be a perfectionist who won't know a moment's peace if he doesn't try to straighten everything he sees that is even slightly out of alignment. He may be arrogant, believing that nothing will ever be right without *his* input. Or he might be a jealous person who nitpicks to keep the person he's jealous of from flying too high. The one thing we can say for sure about nitpickers is that they are morale killers.

Morale is one of the most underrated factors in success. If people are energized and happy and feeling good about how things are going, they are dramatically more effective. This is not just a pop-psychology premise but a fact that has been proven through extensive research. One study by the Wharton Business School revealed that companies with happy employees consistently produce larger returns for their shareholders.[9] At the same time, when people are unhappy, they tend to do the bare minimum and have a higher rate of absenteeism, making success about as likely as the Rock of Gibraltar drifting to Hawaii. I've been on both ends of the morale teeter-totter, and I can tell you that I was a much better pastor when I was up instead of down.

So what do you do if you have a nitpicker in your life?

James 1:19 offers the best answer: "You must all be quick to listen, slow to speak, and slow to get angry."

Be honest. You were hoping for something better than that, weren't you? You were hoping for some tactic, some strategy that would enable you to neutralize this person's negativity. Well, there isn't one. Without some cataclysmic, life-changing spiritual experience, nitpickers are going to nitpick, and there's nothing you can do to stop them. You can try to talk to them and ask them to cool it, but that will likely just redirect their nitpicking. Instead of telling *you* what you're doing wrong, they'll tell *everyone else* what you're doing wrong. It might seem like the situation has improved because the noise in your ear has abated, but it likely hasn't.

I know of no better option than going to your knees and asking God for the strength to live out James 1:19. This verse has been the central text of a million sermons, but sometimes you have to quit talking about it and start living it.

1. *Quick to listen.* Is your nitpicker right about any of the nits he is picking?
2. *Slow to speak.* He may be guilty of the very thing for which he's criticizing you. Just let it go.

3. *Slow to get angry.* You're on your way to becoming a great Christian when you can smile and say thank you to someone you'd prefer to kick in the shins.

When I was twenty-two, I played it just right with the guy who corrected my grammar every week. It wasn't because I was spiritual. It was because I was scared. I smiled and accepted his little sheet of paper because I was trying not to make an enemy in the first month of my new ministry. You might be interested to know that the person who caught and corrected all of my dangling participles is, almost fifty years later, a friend I still hear from. I'm pretty sure our friendship would never have happened if I'd been slow to listen, quick to speak, and quick to get angry.

#22

THE SELF-STOPPER

Every employer loves to hire people who are self-starters. Self-starters don't need someone standing over them, telling them what to do. They can see for themselves what needs to be done and will jump right in and do it. Self-starters aren't people you have to push. If anything, you have to hold them back. But every boss I've ever known would much prefer having employees that have to be held back over those who have to be pushed.

Thankfully, there are self-starters in the church—people who see needs and step right up and meet them. Some of my favorite moments in ministry have been when someone came to my office and said, "Mark, I've noticed that we don't have anybody doing such-and-such. I'd be happy to take on that job if it's okay." Self-starters are a blessing!

Sadly, most churches have as many self-stoppers as self-starters. A self-stopper is a person who never finishes anything. You can recruit him, train him, assign him to his post, and feel like you've really accomplished something. But it won't be long until he's a no-call, a no-show. Of course, he'll give you reasons and apologies and promises to not let it happen again. But it *will* happen again, probably soon, and then a third time after another round of apologies. Eventually, the person won't even bother with the apologies anymore. He'll assume you've figured out that he's not going to continue with his assignment, which is correct. You saw it coming from the first no-call, no-show.

What's truly disappointing about this type of person is that everything is set up for him to succeed. For one thing, most jobs we assign to church members are not difficult. I mean, we're not asking them to perform brain surgery. We're just asking them to wash the baptismal robes or stand at the door and shake hands or direct some cars toward the empty parking spaces. We also offer training and support and often team the new volunteer up with someone who has experience.

Remember when your children were toddlers and you had an Easter egg hunt in your yard? Remember how easy you made it for them? You put them all in plain sight: a pink one right in the middle of the yard, a bright yellow one on the front step, a blue one on the sidewalk leading to the mailbox. This is what we do for most of our volunteers at church. We set it up so there's almost no way they can fail. But they do fail, because they can't get out of their own way. They are *self*-stoppers. Not all self-stoppers are alike, but there are three characteristics they often possess.

1. *A chaotic personal life.* They're often running late, barking at their children, scrambling to cope with whatever task is right in front of them, even if it's something as simple as getting to church on time. They mean well, which is why they want to help out at church, but until they sort out their personal drama and get better organized, they're never going to be able to handle a ministry assignment well.

2. *Low self-esteem.* They're looking for a way to feel better about themselves, so they volunteer to serve. Unfortunately, they quickly realize that performing a small service at church doesn't come close to counterbalancing the reasons why they feel bad about themselves. You can imagine how quickly their enthusiasm for their ministry assignment drains away when they realize it didn't make them feel better after all, although it *did* add one more responsibility to their hectic schedule.

3. *A lack of vision.* Take someone who volunteers to work in the church nursery. It seems like it will be fun—rocking and feeding and playing with the babies. But that assumption is torpedoed in the first ten minutes when three kids are screaming at the same time and a fourth has produced a bowel movement that could well be a world record. It's at that point the volunteer must be able to see beyond the screaming and chaos and stench to the higher purpose of the nursery ministry. Young parents, some of whom may not know Christ, are able to sit in the worship service and hear the word of God preached without the distraction of dealing with their kids. It's no exaggeration to say that eternal salvation could hang in the balance for some of those parents, which makes the work that's being done with their kids in the nursery extraordinarily important. But if the nursery volunteer can't see this bigger vision despite the unpleasantness, it's unlikely he or she will last.

The good news is that self-stoppers are rarely malicious or critical of the church. They know the church gave them an opportunity and tried to help them succeed. They may even love the church more for having been given a chance. But that doesn't minimize the trouble they cause.

When I was a boy, I knew what I could get away with and what I couldn't. I think most kids figure this out pretty quickly. Every parent has buttons, and we quickly learn not to push them. One of my mom's buttons was finding a mess in a place she had just cleaned and straightened. Understandably, it irked her to find that her time and effort had gone for nothing, and that the place looked just like she'd never touched it.

This is the biggest problem with self-stoppers. As a church leader, you think you have someone recruited and trained and plugged in to serve, only to quickly find out you don't. You realize that your time and effort were wasted on that person and that you're going to have to do it all again. I cringe when I think of all the work I *could* have been doing if I hadn't had to spend so much of my ministry time doing the same jobs over and over.

So what's the answer?

Obviously, it would be nice if there was a way to know if a person was a self-stopper before he self-stopped. Toward that end, we can be more thoughtful when we're recruiting people to serve. Sometimes a failure happens on the back end because we aren't careful on the front end. We rush someone into a volunteer position with our fingers crossed when we should be asking questions and looking for signs that he or she isn't right for the job. Yes, I said looking for signs that the person *isn't* right for the job. Typically, we don't look for reasons *not* to assign the person. We're so desperate to get the position filled and move on that we only check and see if a person has a faint pulse. We hold a mirror up to his nose and see if he's breathing. If he is, we sign him up!

Although it took me a number of years, I eventually learned the wisdom of telling a person he isn't a good fit for a volunteer position if all the signs are pointing toward that being the case. You do it nicely, of course. You find him another assignment if you can, one that isn't as critical. Or you ask him to wait until he has some of his life circumstances more settled. Don't create problems for yourself by knowingly driving a square peg into a round hole. No sane business leader would do this, so why should we do it in the church?

We might also retain more people if our expectations of our volunteers were more reasonable. In the typical church, every volunteer ministry is a lifetime appointment. You either have to die or go into witness protection to get rid of the job. That is both unfair and unkind.

In my experience, volunteers are more likely to hang in there if they know the actual day on the calendar when they're going to get a break, and if it's not too far in the future.

Still, no matter how careful and thoughtful leaders are, no matter how hard they work to find the right people, there will always be self-stoppers to drive them crazy, and not just in church. I was in a restaurant recently where the service was atypically poor. As I paid the check, our frazzled server apologized profusely. She said that right before we walked in, one of their recent hires had quit on the spot and marched out the door. They were scrambling to call in a replacement.

I could only smile.

#21

THE FAUCET

In his famous message to the church in Laodicea, Jesus said, "I know all the things you do, that you are neither hot nor cold. I wish that you were one or the other! But since you are like lukewarm water, neither hot nor cold, I will spit you out of my mouth!" (Rev. 3:15–16). With that, Jesus ensured that the temperature metaphor would be the most common way we describe a person's level of spiritual commitment. We talk about someone being "on fire" for the Lord. We say she's really "cooled off" in her commitment. And though I don't have any research to back me up, I would guess that 99.9 percent of all preachers have at least one sermon in the file about the dangers of being lukewarm.

Normally, we think of a person being one of the three: hot, cold, or lukewarm. But there are plenty of Christians who ought to have "Moen" or "Delta" stamped on their foreheads: they are like faucets, running hot one minute and cold the next with a little lukewarmness thrown in from time to time.

I can't address this point without telling you about a couple in one of the churches I served. They sat in the second row, right in front of the pulpit. During the musical portion of the service, they would stand and sing at the tops of their lungs. They clapped and bounced in time with the music. They waved their hands in the air. They were into it 100 percent. Then, when I preached, they hung on every word. They often told me after the service how much they appreciated the message, sometimes even sharing a specific way they would apply it in their lives that coming week.

Then they would disappear.

I don't mean in a puff of smoke, à la David Copperfield. I mean they wouldn't show up at church for months. The first time this happened, I spoke to the wife and asked if she and her husband were okay. She laughed and said, "Oh yes, we just got a little lazy, that's all. We'll be back, don't worry." And they did come back, but it wasn't until about six months later. And yes, you guessed it: They parked themselves in the same seats on the second row and resumed their exuberant worship just like nothing ever happened.

This became such a pattern for that couple that I stopped giving it a second thought when they disappeared. One day a new staff member, who didn't know the couple very well, expressed concern because he hadn't seen them at church in a while. (With their worship style and sitting right in the front, they were hard to miss.) When I said, "They aren't due to come back for about three more months," he gave me a quizzical look and asked, "Where did they go?" "No place," I replied. "They're just going through their cold phase right now."

This type of behavior is not uncommon. Virtually every church has people who run hot and cold. Here are my theories as to why they do.

First, it's possible that *they're not as committed as they seem during their hot periods*. They look super committed when you see them on Sunday, but if you followed them around during the week, you might discover that their everyday behavior looks very different. If true, then this suggests they feel the need to return to church for a while to shed some guilt and get back to feeling spiritual again. Then, once they do, they'll be like a car that's been in the shop for an overhaul: ready to hit the road again.

A second reason why I suspect some people run hot and cold is because *they are fragile emotionally*. If there's one thing I know, it's that it takes very little to derail some Christians. I've had people come to my office to tell me about some catastrophic event that caused them to spiral into a crisis of faith, only to find out when they describe it that it wasn't catastrophic at all. It was actually a small event. A *really* small event you would think any Christian with even a little spiritual muscle would be able to process with no problem. Yes, many Christians are spiritual wimps.

In case you're wondering, no, it's not lost on me that we preachers and teachers might be partly to blame here. Is our preaching and teaching lacking? Are we feeding our people milk toast instead of meat? If so, that could be one reason why they're weak and fragile.

A third reason I think people run hot and cold is simply because *it's part of their personality to do so.* I'm no personality expert, but I've observed that people who run hot and cold at church often run hot and cold in other areas of their lives too. Depending on when you talk to them, they may or may not be going to the gym. They may or may not be looking for a new job. They may or may not be getting along with their spouse.

The reason these human faucets made the list of most troublesome church members is not because they're actively trying to cause trouble, but because their witness stands in opposition to everything the Bible teaches about how to live the Christian life. Paul said, "My dear brothers and sisters, be strong and immovable" (1 Cor. 15:58). The writer of Hebrews told us to hold onto our faith "without wavering" (Heb. 10:23). It's counterproductive to our cause when the lifestyles of church members stand in opposition to the content of our preaching. We wouldn't doubt that this is true if we were preaching about sexual purity and people in the church were openly having affairs, so why would we doubt it if we're preaching about steadfastness and our people are running hot and cold?

There's also the loss of effective influence a church suffers when people run hot and cold. Consistency isn't all that exciting. Although a constant drip, drip, drip is never going to wow anybody, it's how canyons are made.[10] There is far more power in a steady drip than there is in a spigot that's occasionally turned on and off. There is far more power in a Christian who shows up and serves consistently through thick and thin than there is in a Christian who makes a big splash for a while and then disappears for months. It's not just true in church. Ask any coach if he'd rather have a steady, consistent player or one who is super-talented but won't always show up. Ask any business owner if she'd rather have a steady, consistent employee or one who is super-talented but won't always show up. Everything we experience in life screams for the value of being steady and consistent. You won't get it with the faucets.

So what do we do?

For one, we can preach often on themes related to faithfulness and consistency. Although it's wonderful to preach uplifting sermons of comfort and encouragement, we also need to challenge our people. In a culture where we're accustomed to seeing people react harshly to things they don't like, in this age of short fuses when more and more people wear their feelings on their sleeve and push back against anything (or anyone) that makes them uncomfortable, we need to ask ourselves if our preaching has grown soft and safe. Are we afraid to call out our people for their inconsistency? Do we default to topics we know won't ruffle any feathers?

We can also speak one-on-one with those who have this problem and encourage them to take a serious look at their witness, to view it through new eyes. I've seen cases where just being honest with people about their weakness in a particular area helped tremendously. Sometimes they don't realize how significantly their actions are hindering the church. They assume that because they're not actively or intentionally stirring up trouble, they couldn't possibly be considered troublesome. As church leaders, one of our jobs is to help them see what they might be missing.

While writing this chapter about inconsistency, my mind has been flashing back to the early 1980s. I was in my twenties and serving a church that placed a lot of emphasis on Sunday school attendance. When I say "a lot of emphasis," I mean they had cabinets full of attendance registers going back over fifty years and held annual ceremonies where they gave out lapel pins to faithful members who achieved notable attendance milestones. I'll never forget the time a young woman came to Sunday school carrying an empty bowl and a wet cloth pressed to her forehead. She was as sick as a dog but couldn't bear to break her streak of perfect attendance and miss out on getting her next pin.

We could debate the wisdom of this over-the-top emphasis, but it was how things were done in that church and, as a young whippersnapper of a preacher, I kept my mouth shut and went with the flow.

I mention this because there was a member of that congregation who, if he had wanted to, could have worn enough attendance pins to cover his entire suit coat. The man hadn't missed Sunday school in forty-five years. His name was Paul and no, he wasn't a church or community big shot. He was a simple man who worked at a small grocery store a few blocks from the church building. I used to go in there and see him in his white apron, sweeping the floors or stocking the shelves. I don't think I ever saw him when he wasn't smiling.

Here's the most important thing you need to know about Paul: he didn't pile up all those years of perfect attendance for the pins. In fact, though he must've had close to fifty of them, I never saw him wearing one. Whenever they presented him with a new one, he always looked embarrassed. He didn't go to Sunday school every week for almost a half century for the pins. He went for the Lord.

I didn't appreciate it at the time, but Paul was putting forth one of the clearest pictures of faithfulness and consistency a young preacher would ever see. Now that I'm much older and have encountered so many people like the hot-and-cold couple I described at the beginning of this chapter, I realize what a rare and beautiful picture it was.

#20

THE JELLYFISH

The jellyfish is one of the strangest animals on earth in that it has no ears, eyes, nose, brain, or heart. But the reason I chose it to represent #20 on my list of most troublesome church members is because of something else it doesn't have: a backbone. This is why it looks like a pulsating blob compared to other sea creatures.

Metaphorically, the backbone has come to represent courage and strength of character, which is why you'll often hear someone say about a weak or wishy-washy person, "He needs to grow a backbone!" It's also common to hear a strong, determined leader referred to as "the backbone of the organization."

Thankfully, the church has always been full of people with backbones. Think about the courage and strength of character the apostles showed in those early days when being an outspoken follower of Christ could cost you your life. Think of the countless missionaries who have made mind-blowing sacrifices and risked their lives—even *given* their lives—to see that the gospel was carried around the world. Think about the untold number of Christians who get up every day and go to work in environments that are, if not openly hostile, certainly not supportive of their faith and values. Yes, the church is a place where you can find backbones aplenty.

Sadly, it's also a place where you can find jellyfish.

A jellyfish is a spineless person, one who lacks courage and strength of character. He may be very friendly and likable. He might be someone with whom you enjoy going to lunch or playing golf, but when a critical moment comes and a stand needs to be taken for the cause of Christ, he will wobble and waffle until the moment passes. At heart, the jellyfish is a coward, an appeaser, guaranteeing that his tent will always be pitched somewhere along the path of least resistance.

The jellyfish is different from most of the other people on this list in that he made the list not because of what he does, but because of what he doesn't do. Specifically, he doesn't stand up for what's right. When someone whispers a bit of juicy gossip, when someone offers unfair criticism of the church's leaders, when someone disparages the pastor's vision for the future of the church, the jellyfish just sits there. He offers no push back, no opposing point of view, no defense of those being attacked. Even if he strongly disagrees with what's being said, he keeps his mouth shut.

I recall the time a friend of mine reported a particularly nasty criticism he'd heard directed at our church's leadership team. It was both untrue and unkind and, I'll be honest, it hurt. I felt good, however, knowing my friend had been there when the comment was made. I just knew he'd spoken up in our defense, and I couldn't wait to hear what he'd said. But when I asked him, he replied, "I didn't say anything. I wasn't sure what to say. I decided to just tell you about it and let you handle it." A classic jellyfish response.

Can you imagine an army where the soldiers never return the enemy's fire? Picture a G.I. being shot at. He's got a rifle in his hands and knows how to use it; but instead of returning fire, he pulls out a pencil and paper and writes a note to his commander back behind the lines: "Sir, I thought you should know that they're shooting at us out here. I wasn't sure what to do, so I just decided to tell you about it." How would you rate the chances of that commander's army winning the war?

Keeping a church healthy and relatively trouble-free is not something the pastor and leadership team can do alone. Church members must have enough courage and strength of character to respond in the moment. When he heard the untrue and unkind criticism directed at our leadership team, my friend should have spoken right up and said, "I happen to know that's not true. I would encourage you to talk to Mark or one of the elders so you can get the story straight." What a powerful moment that would have been! Such a statement would have struck a blow for truth and righteousness and surely would have had a profound impact on others who were listening.

When writing to the church in Ephesus, Paul said, "Take no part in the worthless deeds of evil and darkness; instead, expose them" (Eph. 5:11). The first part of that verse is pretty easy for most Christians—even jellyfish—to obey. It serves as a kind of "not guilty" plea when trouble surfaces in the church. The jellyfish can say, "It's not my fault. I haven't been taking part in any worthless deeds of evil and darkness!" That may technically be true, as in the case of my friend. After all, he wasn't the one speaking against our leadership team. But the second half of the verse can't be ignored. Failing to speak up and expose gossip, lies, and inaccuracies when the opportunity to do so is wide open makes one an accessory.

I also want to point out Proverbs 31:8: "Speak up for those who cannot speak for themselves." We often think of the unborn or those suffering under the heavy hand of injustice when we think about those who cannot speak for themselves. But do you know who else can't speak for him- or herself? The person who isn't present when a lie or unfair criticism is being leveled. That's why the person who *is* present must do the speaking up.

The question is, can a coward grow a backbone?

The answer is yes. I remember very well the day I grew one.

I was in high school and in love with the girl who would eventually become my wife. One day, a bully who liked to pick on me walked up to me in study hall and grabbed the front of my sweater. He pulled it out about a foot from my body, twisted it hard, and released it. The result was that I looked ridiculous. I had a huge protrusion in the middle of my chest. Of course, my antagonist almost fell down laughing while others seated nearby also laughed.

The reason the kid felt confident enough to do this was because he knew I was a jellyfish. He'd picked on me many times before without getting any push back. This time, however, the situation was different. The girl I was in love with was seated a few feet away, watching.

That was the game changer.

In a flash of insight, I understood that the consequences of not reacting were going to be far greater than anything I might suffer by being brave. So, to the complete surprise of my tormentor, I stepped forward and threw the only punch I've ever thrown in my life. It was a roundhouse right that came up from the floor. Fortunately, he saw it coming and leaned back slightly, causing me to miss his nose by an inch. Immediately, I loaded up for another one, but by then he was backpedaling. I pressed my advantage and was just about to swing again when he turned and ran.

He turned and ran!

He never bothered me again.

Of course, I'm not condoning this type of behavior and was sorry it came to that. But I have to say that this was a transformative moment in my life. It was the moment when I grew a backbone—when I shed my jellyfish persona like a snake sheds its skin. It happened only because I suddenly understood that the cost of being a coward was going to be far greater than the cost of being brave.

As church leaders, this is what we must get across to our people. We pay a very high price when we fail to confront liars and gossips and critics. It feels like the safe choice in the moment, but all it does is give bad people the green light to spread poison throughout the church. Solomon said, "There is a time to be quiet and a time to speak" (Eccl. 3:7). To a significant degree, the health of every church will depend on the ability of its people to figure out which time is which.

#19

THE WRECKING BALL

I got a call one day from a young mom who had three children not yet old enough to go to school. She was sobbing on the phone, making it impossible for me to understand her. Alarmed, I told her I was on my way, hung up the phone, and drove straight to her house. When I arrived, she answered the door with a baby on her hip and a couple of toddlers at her feet. Her eyes were bloodshot from crying, but I was at least happy to see that no one appeared to be physically injured.

When we sat down in her living room, I noticed that all three children had stuffy noses and were out of sorts. They were whining and pawing at their mom, fully engaged in a competition for her attention. She looked exhausted and was dabbing at her bloodshot eyes with a tissue. Clearly, something major had happened.

When I asked why she called, she told me about a visit she'd just had from her neighbor, an older woman she said was extremely religious. The lady apparently knew the kids had been sick for a few days, so she felt compelled to stop by—not to bring a pot of soup or maybe something sweet for the kids to eat—but to tell this frazzled young mom that if she wanted her kids to get better, she needed to repent of her sin. She said God was using the kids' suffering to get her attention, and she challenged the young woman about what she might be doing in her personal life to make God so angry.

I remember being so mad my face felt red hot. If I were going to make a list of the Top 10 angriest moments in my life, that would definitely be one. I wanted to storm across the yard to the older woman's house, bang on her door with both fists, and give her a piece of my mind. Instead, I spent a long time trying to undo the damage the older woman had done.

Say hello to #19 on my list: the wrecking ball.

You've seen a real wrecking ball in action. It knows nothing of softness or gentleness. It crashes into things and causes damage and destruction. If you see a concrete building that has been reduced to a pile of rubble, then you know a wrecking ball has been there. Human wrecking balls do the same thing, only to people.

As a pastor, it strikes me that the woman who was a wrecking ball to that young mom was a member of a church. The following Sunday, I suspect she walked into her church, probably carrying a fifteen-pound Bible, smiling, and greeting her friends. I can just imagine her taking a seat and singing songs of praise, taking Communion, and "amening" her preacher half to death. When the service was over, I have no doubt she waved and hugged her way to her car and drove home feeling like a great Christian, never stopping to think that right next door to her lived a young woman who was deeply wounded because of her heartless and judgmental spirit.

The question is, how did this woman become a wrecking ball? I can think of a couple of possibilities.

One is that *she was raised in a religious tradition that emphasized holiness but rarely, if ever, mentioned grace*. There are churches where people are constantly harangued for sinning. Forget lying and stealing and fornicating. They're told that the wrath of God will fall on them like fire from heaven if they even go to a movie or drink a glass of wine or wear a two-piece bathing suit at the beach. At the same time, they are never reminded that they are saved by grace and that God's grace is greater than their sin (Rom. 5:20–21). Thus they learn to see sin everywhere they look while grace never crosses their minds. If you're a pastor, I plead with you to make sure your preaching is full of truth *and* grace (John 1:14 NIV). Otherwise, your church will likely become a wrecking-ball factory.

There's a second, less obvious possibility as to how this woman became a wrecking ball: *By being conditioned to believe that her church and indeed her style of Christianity is superior to everyone else's.* I learned that the wrecking-ball lady had invited the young mom and her family to her church multiple times; but every time she did, the young woman told her they already had a church they loved. The young mom later told me that when it became obvious that she and her husband weren't going to leave our church, the neighbor woman's attitude became noticeably less congenial—which begs the question: When the neighbor woman pronounced judgment on the young mom and accused her of some hidden sin, was this some kind of warped statement of spiritual superiority? Would she have done such a thing if the young mom had left our church and joined hers? I don't know, of course; but I have a hunch that if that young mom *had* switched churches, she would have gotten the older woman's stamp of approval and received a pot of homemade soup that day instead of a browbeating.

The reason wrecking-ball people are counterproductive to the cause of Christ should be obvious. If it isn't, then simply think about what you would do if you had a condemned building that needed to be knocked down. You wouldn't call a construction company; you would call a demolition crew. The Bible clearly states that the church is supposed to be about construction and building, not demolition and tearing down (Eph. 4:12). I'd say it's impossible to remind people of this too often, especially in a culture where tearing people down is a national pastime. It is to our shame if we allow this kind of behavior to go on in the church.

I want you to know that thirty-five years later, that young mom, whom I hadn't seen or talked to in over thirty years, sent me a message and reconnected with me. I was thrilled to learn that those three little tykes, whose noses she had wiped on that eventful day, had made her a grandmother. Even more, I was delighted to hear that she had remained faithful to the Lord and was happily serving in her church. There was no word, however, on what ever happened to the wrecking ball next door. I hope everyone survived her crashes as well that young mom.

#18

THE WHINER

On October 11, 1975, *Saturday Night Live* premiered on NBC. Driven by comedy skits that parody pop culture and politics, the show has won countless awards and turned a lot of obscure comedians into household names. Back in the 1980s, *SNL* regulars Joe Piscopo and Robin Duke created a couple of memorable characters named Doug and Wendy Whiner. Doug and Wendy were, well, whiners. In every skit, no matter where they went, no matter what they did, they found something to whine about. I recall seeing a clip of them in a fancy French restaurant. They took one look at the menu and said to the server in their typical whiney, sing-song voice, "We can't eat this *stuuuuff*. We have *diverticuliiiiitis*. Do you have any macaroni and *cheeeeeeeeeese*?"

Every church I've ever served has had a Doug or a Wendy, or a Doug *and* a Wendy Whiner. Some have had several. Here are some of the more common whines I've heard over the years.

"The music is too loud!" This was the mantra of a lady who would sit with her fingers in her ears throughout the music portion of the service. Afterward, she would complain about the volume even though, for her sake, we purchased and used a decibel meter and kept the sound in the "comfortable" range. When we realized that she whined just as much when we used the decibel meter as she did when we didn't use it, we quit using it.

"We don't sing enough hymns!" This is another classic whine I've heard a thousand times. I'll never forget the Sunday someone put an anonymous note in the offering plate, informing us that it had been "weeks" since we had sung a hymn when, in fact, that

very Sunday we had sung three hymns. Either the person had slept through the service or didn't recognize the hymns when they were done in a more contemporary style.

"We don't sing enough of the newer songs!" Yes, the whines cut both ways when it comes to music. There were actually times when, on the same day, we got complaints about not singing enough hymns *and* not singing enough new songs!

"I don't like the new order of worship!" Not one single time did we ever make a change to our regular order of worship without hearing from the whiners. When we put the Lord's Supper before the sermon, people said they couldn't worship unless it was after the sermon. When we put it after the sermon, people said they couldn't worship unless it was before the sermon. Some even threatened to find another church if the situation wasn't "corrected." Once, when I started delegating the opening welcome announcement to our female worship leader, we actually had people complain that this didn't seem right when it wasn't done by the senior pastor.

There are three things that make whiners especially frustrating.

1. *They always seem to be hung up on things that are of little or no importance.* Pastors and other church leaders are trying to figure out how to manage the budget and minister to the needy and reach the lost, while the whiner seems obsessed with whether the Lord's Supper is served at 10:15 or 10:45 on Sunday morning. Whiners often seem like the kind of people who would complain about the pictures on the wall being crooked when the house is on fire.

2. *Whiners are completely inward focused.* Everything we preach and teach about how to live the Christian life relates in some way to being selfless and generous and willing to sacrifice. But whiners don't seem to be able to see beyond their own likes and dislikes. It's not what's good for the church, but what's good for them that consumes their thoughts.

3. *Whiners delight in broadcasting their displeasure.* This is a particularly uncomfortable truth in a social-media driven world. In the old days, whiners told their pew mates and maybe a couple of close friends how they felt. Now they can pull out their phones and tell the whole world. I have cringed (and fumed) at some of the whiney, self-centered, small-minded social media posts I've seen.

Based on my experience, church leaders are wise to do the following with whiners.

First, *ignore their complaints.* Notice that I didn't say to ignore *them*, just their complaints. You make a huge mistake if you let gripey, whiney people start dictating what you do. When you cater to whiners, you're actually building a culture where whiners can thrive. As the old saying goes: Whatever behavior you reward, you get more of. Of course, you're thinking, "But wait, Mark. What if one of them has a legitimate complaint?" Believe me, if the complaint is legitimate, then you're going to be hearing it from non-whiners too. Any complaint you get that's *only* coming from a whiner is likely nothing to worry about.

Second, *take the high road.* When you see that one of your whiners has posted something negative about you or your church on social media, the temptation to add your own comment as a rebuttal will be strong. Don't do it, for two reasons. One, you will look small and thin-skinned. And two, you will run the risk of escalating the situation. You don't have to read through very many social media threads to learn that they can get ugly pretty quickly. Don't let yourself be connected to something like that. Besides, the whiner would probably love it if you jumped into the fray. It would tell him that he got under your skin.

If we're honest, we have to admit that there's a little whiner in all of us. We come out of the womb screaming for what we want and against what we don't want. Then, as toddlers, we whine so much that someone dubbed that period of our lives "the terrible twos." Even when we grow up and gain some spiritual maturity, we can still have our moments. And yes, that goes for pastors. I've known pastors who could whine with as much proficiency as Pavarotti singing opera. So, when you encounter a whiner in your church and you feel that churning in your gut, let it be your reminder not to be that way yourself.

#17

THE VAMPIRE

When I was eleven years old, an afternoon soap opera called *Dark Shadows* made its television debut. In many respects, it was just like any other soap opera. It focused on the relationships and problems of a wealthy family and the various eccentric characters in the family's orbit. What set the series apart is that one of the main characters was a vampire. The world was accustomed to soap operas where doctors and nurses cavorted about in hospitals, but a vampire prowling the shadowy halls of a creepy mansion really set people buzzing and made the show enormously popular. The vampire's name was Barnabas Collins. In the first episode of the second season, he was unwittingly released from a chained coffin where he'd been imprisoned for two hundred years. You can imagine how out of sorts he was after being cooped up for so long.

Having a vampire among your circle of acquaintances really complicates your life. If you don't believe me, watch a few reruns of *Dark Shadows*.

Or you could just ask a preacher.

Preachers know all about vampires because they exist in every church. I'm referring to that person who sucks not your blood but every ounce of your energy. He takes advantage of your good will, your patience, and your desire to help. He worms his way into your life and monopolizes your time and attention. He calls you at all hours, drops in unexpectedly, and leaves messages on your phone. When you bump into him at the grocery store, he'll bend your ear for twenty minutes right there in the toilet paper aisle, never stopping to think you might have other things to do. At church, he'll literally stalk you. He'll prowl the hallways until he finds you, and then he'll drone on and on even though there are other people waiting to speak to you.

The vampire is more than just an annoyance—he is a manipulator. You'll discover this if you ever try to create some distance between the two of you. If, for example, you don't answer every call, or if you dare to tell him he shouldn't call you as often, he'll play the martyr. He'll question your compassion. And if you don't yield to his will, he will turn against you.

I'll never forget the day I received a phone call from a fellow staff member at our church. With an urgent tone, he told me to jump online and check out the social media page of one of our members. When he said the name, I cringed, knowing that what I was about to see was not going to be good. The individual was a classic vampire who'd been driving me crazy and from whom I'd been trying to distance myself. Sure enough, when I got to his web page, I read a post that was demeaning of me and our church. Basically, it said that we talked a good game, but we didn't really care about people.

I took a deep breath and let it out slowly.

Then I counted to ten.

Then I reflected on all the time and attention I'd given this man. I'd spent hours with him and had even used my influence to get him some financial assistance when he was without a job. I knew that a couple of men in our church had done some house repairs for him free of charge, and that an older lady in our church had let him use her car when his was in the shop. But he still told the world that we were all talk and didn't really care about people.

Then I counted to twenty because ten wasn't enough.

The jury is still out when it comes to the question of whether vampires have serious personal issues or are just immature. Those who vote for immaturity point out that vampires do many of the things a small child would do. Picture a diaper-clad toddler following its mother around the house, holding up its arms, whining and begging to be held, and then throwing a tantrum when Mommy doesn't respond. Vampires do the same thing, only without the diaper. But I'll leave the analysis to the experts. My concern here is the damage such people do.

- Yes, they eat up your time.
- Yes, they frustrate you.
- Yes, they make you want to peek around corners before you walk down a hallway just to make sure they aren't there.
- And yes, they make you angry enough to spit when they eventually turn on you.

The worst thing people like this do is harden your heart. A Christian, especially a pastor, needs a tender, breakable heart in order to do the work of Christ well. But doing your very best to help someone and then having that person blame you for not doing even more makes you cynical. Maybe not so much the first time it happens, but as the experience repeats itself—and it always does—your spirit hardens.

Perhaps you've noticed that some pastors, usually middle-aged or older, are a bit sarcastic or smart-alecky when talking about the ministry in general and people in particular. I once heard a pastor say from his pulpit during a Sunday morning service, "I preach for free. It's putting up with you people I get paid for." People in the audience didn't know if he was joking or serious—but I knew him well and believe me, he was serious.

I only know of one answer for combating this cynicism: prayer. I know, I know, it's such a cliché. It's like the little kid in Sunday school. He doesn't know the answers to the Bible questions the teacher is asking, but he figures he can't go too far wrong if he just says "Jesus" every time. It's the same with prayer. It always seems to be the recommendation. Then again, maybe that's because it's always the best option.

I'm thinking of the prayer David offered in Psalm 139. In verses 23 and 24, he says, "Search me, O God, and know my heart; test me, and know my anxious thoughts. Point out anything in me that offends you." I know of no better way to keep from growing cynical than to pray that prayer from the heart every day. I'll admit there were many times I needed to pray it but was too busy nursing my anger and frustration. That's the challenge. It *feels* better to nurse our feelings than to lay our hearts open to God and ask him to come in and have a look around. Although prayer may be the simple answer, it's not always the easy one.

It would be so nice if we could solve vampire problems simply by waving a crucifix or maybe sticking a few cloves of garlic in our pockets. While chaining them up in coffins for two hundred years may seem extreme, there have been days when I would have voted for it. But since those options aren't available to us, we need to do what we always need to do when we encounter people problems: look first at ourselves. If we keep our own heads and hearts straight, we may still feel frustrated at times, but we won't diminish ourselves and our effectiveness by allowing the poison of cynicism to seep in.

#16

THE BFF WANNABE

I grew up the son of a barber and a secretary. We were never rich. The houses we lived in, the cars we drove, and the clothes we wore were perfectly ordinary. I was a decent student, an okay athlete, and possessed average looks. I had friends but never an entourage. I went on dates, but I never needed a little black book to keep my girlfriends organized. I was the kind of person most people didn't notice.

All of that changed when I became a preacher.

Suddenly, eyes were on me, people were interested in me, and many of them wanted to be my friend. What bothered me was that a few of them made it clear that they were determined to be my *best* friend. My BFF, if you will. Two incidents stand out.

The first occurred several decades ago, long before cellphones and computers. It was my first Christmas with the church I was serving. An elder and his wife dropped by our house with gifts. One smallish gift would have seemed thoughtful and sweet, but they came marching into our home with their arms loaded. I remember being shocked at the number of presents, but not half as shocked as when I saw what was inside the wrapped boxes: a Kodak Super-8 movie camera, a projector, several rolls of film, a collapsible movie screen, and numerous toys and stuffed animals for our infant daughter. They clearly had spent hundreds of dollars—in today's money, probably over a thousand. We were speechless. It seemed wildly over the top. Not even our parents gave us such extravagant gifts.

Feeling uneasy, I shared what happened with an older, wiser pastor. He said, "All of that stuff was a down payment on your friendship. They were staking their claim, letting you know that they expect to be your best friends."

Fast-forward ten years.

We moved to another town where I became the pastor of a different church. After the very first Sunday evening service, a man—again, an elder—and his wife hung around and talked to my wife and me after everyone else had gone home. They told us that they had a special place in their hearts for pastors and that they had been best friends with all of the congregation's recent pastors. They told story after story about the great times they had had with them—vacations they had taken together, backyard barbecues and double dates and ballgames and movie nights. Feeling uneasy, we listened and smiled and nodded. The same thing was happening again. The couple was obviously letting us know that they expected us to be their best friends. (Later that night, we jokingly agreed that we liked it better when people laid claim to BFF status *with* gifts rather than without.)

As almost everyone knows, a deep friendship can't be forced. It must happen naturally. It's most likely to happen when two people have compatible personalities, shared values, common experiences, and a similar worldview. But even then, it doesn't always work. The mysterious "click" two people have to experience in order to become best friends is impossible to predict. The one thing we do know is that it can't be manufactured at will.

So, of course, you're wondering what happened between us and those two couples. And you're probably wondering why they made this list at #16. After all, just wanting to be someone's best friend seems harmless, right?

Think again.

We didn't click with either of these couples. The main reason was because they tried too hard. Have you ever conversed with a loud talker who got right in your face? Didn't he make you want to lean back and step away to preserve your personal space? That's how we felt with these couples. They came on too strong, and we found ourselves leaning away from them instead of toward them. And no, they didn't take kindly to losing the BFF Sweepstakes, which was bad news for us because of both men's status as elders.

With the couple who gave us all the gifts on our first Christmas, the relationship was testy. With the second couple, the one who informed us that they had been best friends with all the church's recent preachers, our relationship was a complete disaster. When it became apparent that we were not going to pal around with them and have backyard cookouts on holidays, they decided they didn't like us at all. Space does not permit me to share all the things they did in an effort to make me look bad. Suffice it to say, I couldn't say or do anything without the two of them being critical. And because of the husband's position of authority, he had more than the usual amount of influence. I didn't last long in that church, and they are the main reason. I have no doubt they celebrated my resignation and started gearing up immediately to make their pitch for BFF status to the next pastor.

It always seemed to me that those couples, especially the one that declared war on us, were insecure. It wasn't me they were desperate to be best friends with. I was just a thirty-something no-name pastor. No, it was my title. It was friendship with *the pastor*—whoever that might be—that was important to them. Somehow, they felt validated if the local "man of God" thought they were wonderful.

Over the years, I learned to be wary of people who needed something from me in order to feel good about themselves. I eventually figured out that if they needed unusually large doses of my time, attention, or friendship in order to be happy with themselves (or with me), then our relationship was destined to end up in a dark place. I have always felt—and I think most pastors would agree—

that it's hard enough to keep my own head in a good place without having to be responsible for someone else's self-image and happiness. That's a responsibility I can't handle. Thankfully, God never asked me to.

There are different schools of thought regarding pastors and their relationships within the congregation. Some say pastors shouldn't play favorites, that they should treat everybody the same and not have close friends. Others say that, like Jesus, a pastor needs an inner circle of people who are his closest friends and confidants. I never quite figured all of that out. My approach was simply to let my relationships grow (or not grow) naturally. I never tried to manufacture a friendship, yet somehow I ended up with lots of wonderful friends. Perhaps I could have done it all differently, but I'm pretty happy with the end result.

PART TWO

THE DANGEROUS

Dragons are best known for what comes out of their mouths. At times their mouths are flame throwers; other times the heat and smoke are not apparent, but the noxious gas does the damage. Their tongues may be smooth, but they are usually forked.[11]

Marshall Shelley, *Well-Intentioned Dragons*

#15

THE GLORY HOUND

Jesus talked about how the Pharisees routinely blew trumpets to call attention to their benevolent acts, and how they liked to stand on street corners and pray in a loud voice so the passersby could hear them. He said that whatever glory they got in those moments would be all they would ever get (Matt. 6:1–6). The Pharisees were classic glory hounds, a term used for people who want to be noticed and admired.

In one church I served, there was a glory hound who had perfected the art of calling attention to his benevolent acts. No, he didn't hire a trumpet player to follow him around and play "Boogie-Woogie Bugle Boy" every time he helped someone, but he might as well have. Whenever we had a visiting missionary speak at our church, he would wait until after the service when the missionary was standing in the lobby talking to a group of church members. Then he would walk up, excuse himself for butting in, and pull out his wallet, saying something like this: "I put some money in the offering plate, but the Lord is telling me to do more." Then he would pull two or three one hundred dollar bills out of his wallet and hand them to the missionary as the bystanders' eyes popped wide open.

I saw him do this multiple times, and it always made my blood boil. Not the gift, but the timing of it. He could easily have waited until the crowd thinned out and given the money privately, which would have been in line with Jesus' words in the passage cited above: "Don't do your good deeds publicly to be admired by others."

Believe it or not, he was not the biggest glory hound I ever met. That title is actually shared by two people I encountered very early in my ministry when I worked part time at a church while still a student. They were young women from prominent church families who carried on an intense rivalry as vocalists. Long before anyone had even thought of *American Idol*, these two young women carried on a competition that was truly a thing to behold—but not in a good way. If one sang in church one week, the other would sing the next. If one sang a dramatic, emotional song, the other would try to top it with a more dramatic and emotional song. If one hit a high note at the end of her selection, the other would hit a higher note the next week. And in case you think I'm exaggerating I'll tell you that I never saw one girl clap for the other. Not once. They both sat there straight-faced, staring holes into the carpet while the other was singing. In fact, the girls' mothers looked miserable too, like they needed to chug a bottle of Pepto-Bismol while the other girl was singing. I also never saw the girls or their families enjoying a friendly conversation, even though it seemed like they ought to have a lot in common.

Obviously, pride and insecurity formed the foundation upon which that silly competition rested. And "silly" is exactly how the other church members thought of it. Everyone was aware of the rivalry (you couldn't miss it), and no one saw the point of it. What's the big deal if you're the best singer in a church where there are only three or four singers and all of them are amateurs?

But there was an even bigger issue that caused a lot of the eye-rolling among the folks in the congregation, and that is that neither girl was an exceptional singer. They were both confident and loud, but confidence and volume do not a Grammy winner make. The diva-like attitude these girls projected was far greater than their talent level—which, I have found, is common among glory hounds. They are generally far more impressive in their own eyes than in anyone else's.

At this point, you may be wondering why I listed the glory hound at #17. They may produce lots of eye-rolls, but are they really dangerous? Before I answer this question, consider a couple of facts.

First, *in his teaching, Jesus targeted showboating.* He talked a lot about how important it is to do things quietly and humbly. And he tangled with the Pharisees again and again, calling them out repeatedly for being such hot dogs.

Second, in the early days of the church, *God actually struck a couple dead because of an ego-driven maneuver designed to bring them personal glory.* I'm referring to Ananias and Sapphira, who sold a piece of property and told everyone that they gave all of the proceeds to the church when they actually kept some for themselves. To many, this would qualify as a relatively harmless lie since it wasn't directed at another person. It was what many would call a "victimless" sin. Yet the apostle Peter, who confronted Ananias and Sapphira, said, "Why have you let Satan fill your heart? You lied to the Holy Spirit and kept some of the money for yourself" (Acts 5:3). In his mind (and in God's), they had committed an extremely serious sin. Serious enough that it cost them their lives.

So why are glory hounds bad for the church?

Because when our religion becomes a performance intended to entertain or impress people, it's no longer about Christ and, therefore, no longer Christian. It can so easily become a performance. Pastor Tom Hovestol was right when he said, "Religion has far more fans who pay far more money and who are far more serious than circus promoters could ever hope for. No athletic contest, no entertainment spectacle, no political gathering compares to the show that religion regularly parades."[12]

Have you ever seen a picture of a boy lifting up the tent flap to sneak a peek at what's going on under the big top? I often think that Jesus must feel like that boy: on the outside looking in, watching the church's grand spectacle of religious performers doing their tricks and flips and basking in the applause while barely giving him a thought. Imagine someone driving home from church feeling exhilarated, not because a profound truth was received during the sermon or the Holy Spirit touched her heart, but because she nailed that last high note and one-upped the girl who sang last week.

We could call such an attitude many things, but Christian is not one of them.

That's not all. When people are competing for *ooh*s and *ahh*s, there is an undercurrent of jealousy that poisons the church's culture. You get lots of fake smiles and snide remarks made behind their backs. I recall a Sunday when one of the young women I mentioned earlier sang a song at the church's Christmas Eve service. The mother of the other girl, who was upset that *her* daughter wasn't asked to sing, said, "The song was okay, but that dress was hideous. I can't believe she wore something like that."

When I was leading a church, I was adamant that big-ego people who craved attention would not be allowed on the stage or into positions of leadership. Yes, it cost us some talent. There were a few excellent singers and musicians, who came waltzing in like they were God's gift to music sent to make something of our poor little church. They expected to be put on stage immediately, and when it didn't happen, they were gone, off in search of a church that *would* let them perform. I've also known gifted teachers and would-be leaders who quickly vanished when it became apparent that they weren't going to be immediately installed in the exalted position they craved.

Some may disagree, but I always preferred to have humble people with mediocre talent serving in our church rather than big-talent people with egos to match. Maybe our services weren't as slick and flashy as some other churches, but making humility a priority was the only way I knew to make sure Jesus didn't get elbowed out of the way. I never wanted our church to become the big top that Jesus had to lift the flap and peek into.

#14

THE BIG BROTHER

In 1949, George Orwell published a novel now considered a classic: *1984*. Simply put, it is a dystopian novel about the government's ability to control people and behavior. "Big Brother" is the leader of the controlling "Party" that employs thought police to keep people from thinking for themselves or expressing any kind of individuality. The interesting thing about Big Brother is that he may not even exist. No one knows if he is a real person or just an idea propagated to instill fear in people and keep them in line.

It's surprising how Orwellian some churches can be. In John 8:36, Jesus said, "If the Son sets you free, you are truly free." And Paul echoed, "Christ has truly set us free" (Gal. 5:1). Over a dozen times in the New Testament, we're encouraged to relish our freedom in Christ. But there are always Big Brother types who feel that God has called them to police the congregation and make sure everybody toes the line. What line? Big Brother's line, of course. He or she decides where that line should be and draws it, and may God help anyone who doesn't conform.

Many years ago, when one of the churches I served was still small, I happened to be talking to one of our church ladies before a Sunday evening service. She was our resident Big Brother, a kind of self-appointed church cop who was always complaining to me about one person or another in the congregation she thought wasn't doing religion right. (Half the time, *I* was the object of her complaints!) As we chatted, we both saw a young woman walk in and take a seat in the back row. Neither of us had ever seen her before. I was delighted to have a visitor and decided to go over and say hello before the service started.

That's when the unthinkable happened.

The young woman kicked off her flip-flops and curled her legs up underneath her to get more comfortable.

The lady standing beside me gasped. Wide-eyed, she looked at me and said, "Would you look at her! Who does she think she is, coming in here and disrespecting the house of God! I'm going to go over there and tell her to put her shoes on and sit up straight!"

I gently grabbed the woman's arm as she started to storm across the room. She glared at me. I released her arm and said, "Please don't do that. This is obviously her first time here. The last thing we want to do is jump on her two minutes after she walks in the door. Who knows, maybe she's never been to church before. Why don't we just be thankful she's here and let her sit however she feels comfortable?"

Thankfully, Big Brother was able to calm herself and leave the young woman alone. But I noticed she gave her the side-eye all evening. The end of the story is that the young woman was married and had two small children. She had come to that service by herself to check us out. She was quite pleasant and enjoyed the service. The following Sunday, she showed up with her husband and kids, and they attended our church faithfully for a year or so until they moved.

But what would have happened if I hadn't been standing right beside Big Brother when the young woman curled her feet up underneath her? Obviously, she would have pounced—and she would *not* have been kind in doing so. I suspect the young woman would have left, never to return, and would have told all her friends what an unpleasant experience she had at our church. *That* is why Big Brother lands at #14 on this list.

At the core of Big Brother's judgmental spirit is a misunderstanding of the difference between unity and uniformity. Unity is a good thing; every church needs it. Uniformity is a bad thing and is one of the surest ways to ensure a church fails in its mission.

Unity is rooted in our common bond in Christ. We've been cleansed by his blood and are saved. We're members of the same family, on the same team, headed in the same direction—however you want to say it. Uniformity, on the other hand, is all about conforming to a set of expectations that has nothing to do with our allegiance to Christ but everything to do with Big Brother's personal opinions.

I recall a young woman who was new in our church joining our coed softball team. I didn't know her well at all, but I noticed she always wore long sleeves and long pants. One Sunday afternoon, we were playing in ninety-five-degree heat with a scorching sun and not a whiff of breeze. The girl was so hot, she looked like she was about to pass out. I pulled her aside and asked if she was okay. I said, "Maybe some shorts and short sleeves would help you stay a little cooler on these brutally hot days." She gave me an odd look and whispered, "Pastor, I have tattoos on my arms and legs, and I have learned the hard way that some Christians don't take kindly to people with tattoos." I knew in that moment that she had met Big Brothers in whatever churches she had previously attended. In fact, I suspected the reason she started attending our church was because she was looking for a church that wouldn't condemn her because she had tattoos. It broke my heart to think she was scared to let us see that she had them.

In his book *Accidental Pharisees*, Pastor Larry Osborne writes:

> We become accidental Pharisees when we lay down boundary markers that are narrower than the ones laid down by Jesus and then treat people who line up on the wrong side of *our* markers as if they were spiritual imposters or enemies of the Lord. Boundary markers that are narrower than the ones Jesus laid down don't *protect* the flock; they *divide* the flock.[13]

He's right. People are not stupid. When they see that they're being pressured to conform to narrow, opinion-based expectations, they'll pull away.

So what do you do with the Big Brother in your church?

I'm not sure there's a perfect answer to this question. Religion seems to breed people who like to tell everyone else how to live out their faith, which means you're never going to rid your church of them. My approach was to preach often about the freedom we have in Christ and what an awful thing legalism is. I spent a lot of time preaching out of the Gospels, partly because I love Jesus' teachings and parables so much—but also because it's in the Gospels that we see Jesus tangling with the Pharisees, the Big Brothers of their day. It's also in the Gospels that we see Jesus showing grace to people like the woman at the well or the woman caught in the act of adultery. Such people would never pass muster with the Big Brothers who patrol the hallways of our church buildings, but Jesus loved them.

So often, when dealing with troublesome church members, the best thing you can do is lift up Jesus and hope people can see the difference between what is and what should be.

#13

THE SNIPER

Chris Kyle is the most famous sniper in US military history. His fame comes from the fact that he has registered more kills than any other sniper, but also because he wrote a bestselling book about his experiences, which Clint Eastwood then turned into a hit movie. People have a wide range of feelings about snipers. Some say they're murderers, pure and simple. Others argue that they save far more lives than they take by eliminating bad guys and terrorists. You can decide for yourself. My purpose is simply to point out that you don't have to go to a war zone to find a sniper. All you have to do is go to church.

There are people in almost every church who love to take long-distance shots at the pastor or the leadership. Their shots usually come in a couple of different ways.

The first is the cutting remark made *when the person being criticized is not present*. I recall a woman walking up to me one day and asking, "Why do you dislike women?" I would have been less surprised if she'd walked up and punched me in the nose. I said, "Excuse me?" She repeated her question, and I replied, "What makes you think I dislike women?" She then informed me that a certain woman in the church had commented to a group of ladies at a social event that I obviously didn't like women. As soon as she said the name, the pieces fell into place. The woman who had taken the long-distance shot at me had recently been talked to by the elders for stirring up some trouble. She blamed me for her reprimand because I was the one who brought the trouble to the elders' attention. She could have taken responsibility for causing the trouble in the first place, but I guess blaming me seemed to her like the better option. Her response was to put me in her crosshairs and start taking shots from afar.

The other way snipers in the church take their shots is *through anonymous notes and letters.* The anonymous part is what's interesting. I would estimate that the majority of the snarky, anonymous notes and letters our ministry team received over the years were easily identifiable by the handwriting. People forget that in the everyday life of the church, they fill out forms, write checks, sign up for events, and share prayer requests on pew cards. They would be shocked to know how adept the church staff becomes at identifying their handwriting. There were many occasions when we received an unsigned message and knew exactly who wrote it. I always pictured those snipers sitting at home, feeling proud of themselves for being so sneaky—not realizing we knew exactly who they were.

There's another side to knowing your sniper's identity, which gets to the heart of why a sniper is dangerous. It's not just the hurtful things they say, which are bad enough. It's that on those occasions when you know who's shooting at you, you have to process that information in a Christ-honoring way, which isn't easy because Satan always creeps in and whispers little comments into your ear:

- "That person is your enemy."
- "That person is trying to undermine your ministry."
- "That person is talking you down every chance they get."
- "You need to avoid contact as much as you can."
- "You need to watch out for their friends, too. They've probably been told all kinds of negative stuff about you."

Just that quickly, a single comment someone made about you turns into a full-blown conspiracy theory in your mind, affecting how you feel about a person God has entrusted to your care. Suddenly, it's difficult to meet that person in the hallway on Sunday, or to work on the same ministry project. You see the person standing in the corner talking quietly to someone, and you wonder if they're talking about you. If the person does happen to say something nice to you, you write it off, telling yourself that it means nothing and that the person is a hypocrite.

It gives me no pleasure to admit that I have had this experience. I have allowed a sniper shot to get me off-track spiritually. Even when I haven't known for sure who fired the shot, I tried to read between the lines to figure out who my enemy was. I'm sure I've been wrong a few times and ended up resenting someone who was totally innocent.

So let me share what I have learned.

First, *sniper shots should be taken seriously*. They are sinful, a blow to morale, and a threat to the spiritual health of the church.

Second, *sniper shots should not be taken too seriously*. Sound like a contradiction? Let me explain. A certain number of sniper shots are what might be compared to a gun being fired into the air. The sound is loud, perhaps even frightening, but the shot was never intended to hurt or kill. Sometimes people say things they clearly shouldn't say, but they don't really mean any harm. They're not trying to hurt you or undermine your ministry, even though it might seem like it in the moment. The key is to discern whether the round was fired at your heart or over your head.

Always remember that most of the people who attend your church are basically harmless and mean well. They're not out to get you. Sometimes people just love to complain and don't realize how hurtful some of their comments may sound. I've actually known situations where people said hurtful things and later, when they were called on it, didn't even remember what they said. Some people just run their mouths out of habit and truly mean no harm. I'm not defending them; just pointing out why it's good not to overreact.

Third, *the sniper you need to take most seriously is the one who keeps firing*. This is basically how you tell the difference between the sniper who can be ignored and the one who can't. If a wild shot whistles over your head, so be it. That's life. But if someone is using you for target practice, then it's time to take action. The Bible is specific about how to confront someone, which I'll be talking about in Part Four of this book. For now, let me just say that before you confront someone, you must be sure you have the right person. There's a reason why I'm calling them snipers. They like to fire from cover and hide. You might think you know who's pulling the trigger, but don't take action until you're 100 percent sure.

I'll wrap this up by saying that if you have a sniper, you're in good company. Paul had people saying he was weak and his speeches were worthless (2 Cor. 10:10). Jesus was criticized for who he hung out with (Mark 2:15), and his disciples took fire for not washing their hands before eating (Mark 7:5).

I recall a *Far Side* cartoon that showed two deer standing in the forest. One of them has what looks like a target on his chest. The other deer is looking at it and says, "Bummer of a birthmark, Hal." When you step into a position of leadership in the church, you must accept the fact that you have a target on you. Handling the incoming fire wisely will honor God, earn you respect, and prolong your ministry.

#12

THE POLITICAL OPERATIVE

I've always had an interest in politics. I've watched the news and kept myself informed, but I've always made it a priority to keep politics out of my preaching and teaching. There are three reasons for this. First and foremost, I do not believe politicians, political parties, or political platforms are the answer to the world's problems. I think they are the *cause* of a lot of our problems, but not the answer. Second, I don't believe there is any political party that gets it right all the time. God's word does get it right all the time, and so that's what I preach. And third, political talk is divisive. No matter how careful you are, no matter how lightly you step, you *will* make people angry if you start talking politics. I always figured ministry was hard enough without ticking off half of my congregation.

However, I know that many people believe pastors should be taking stands on political issues. Several years ago, back when I cared what people said on social media, I saw a post from a Christian friend who was not a pastor. He wrote: "I blame pastors for a lot of the mess that America is in today. Cowardly pastors ought to be ashamed for not taking a stand on the great political issues of our time."

The post troubled me, so I wrote him a private message. Very kindly, I asked him to rethink his post. I reminded him that when a pastor preaches the gospel, he is stating and defending a set of truths that has resulted in countless millions of people being persecuted or killed. In light of that, is it really fair to call any preacher of the gospel a coward? Plus, I suggested that any true preacher of the complete gospel of Jesus Christ actually *does* address all of the issues central to our nation's struggle, but it's because he doesn't use political buzzwords or endorse candidates that political hard-liners think he's being soft. My friend politely thanked me for my thoughts, but I noticed the tone of his posts didn't change.

Reasonable people can disagree on whether a pastor ought to talk politics from the pulpit, but I suspect most church leaders would agree that a church member who is an outspoken political partisan is going to be trouble. It doesn't matter if he's liberal or conservative; what matters is if he is loud.

I'm thinking of a man obsessed with politics who attended the church I was serving. His obsession was indicated by the bumper stickers on his car, by the political T-shirts he wore, and by the fact that he injected politics into just about every conversation. He often greeted me on Sunday morning with a comment about something that had happened on the political scene that week. I always shook his hand, smiled, and said, "I'm not here to talk about politics; I'm here to worship." You'd think such a response would clue him in to the fact that I didn't want to discuss politics at church, but it didn't. A week or two later, we would do the same little dance all over again. In fact, there were Sundays when I avoided him because something had happened in the political world that week and I knew he would be on fire about it.

Now, you might think that such a person would be annoying but hardly dangerous.

Not true.

This man was a problem because he had no sense of what was inappropriate. For example, I was leading an adult Bible study one day on the subject of truth. I was talking about the damage a lie can do when he suddenly piped up and started railing about what a liar the president was and what damage was being done to our country. I quickly jumped in and said, "Please. Don't inject politics into this Bible study. We're not here for that." I moved on with the lesson, but I could tell that others in the class were steaming.

On another occasion, a lady marched up to me, fuming. Someone had put some political flyers in our Welcome Center, right alongside the brochures for our church. She waved one in front of my face and demanded an explanation. She had heard me say that our church was about Jesus, not politics, and the presence of those partisan flyers alongside our church literature seemed like a contradiction. I took one look at the flyer and instantly knew who was responsible. I thanked her for calling this to my attention and told her I would take care of it. Immediately, I went to the Welcome Center, gathered up the flyers, and dropped them in the recycle bin.

It would be helpful for us to remember that Jesus was about as far from a modern politician as you can get. Politicians today are all about votes; and to get votes they make deals, often lowering their standards and compromising their convictions. They hold $1,000-a-plate dinners in swanky hotels, taking money from special interest groups that expect a quid pro quo. They make wild promises they know they'll never be able to keep. They take polls that help them shape their speeches according to what people say they want. They even do focus groups to discover what specific words people respond to the most.

Can you imagine Jesus doing any of this? He presented himself to the world as a humble servant, possessing only the clothes on his back. He never took a poll to see how he might need to tweak his message to get more followers. He didn't cater to the elite. He didn't hold fundraisers. He never compromised. And he never promoted political solutions to the problems of the day. The kingdom he promoted was spiritual (see John 18:36), which is why some people grew disillusioned with him. They *wanted* him to be political, and he disappointed them.

No two churches are alike, so I suppose there are churches where a political operative like I have described in this chapter would fit right in. But mostly, such a person is going to irritate people and possibly even drive them away. Remember that it doesn't matter whether your political operative is liberal or conservative—half your church is going to be what he isn't and is going to experience a slow burn when he starts mouthing off. As a church member once said to me, "If church is just going to be more of the same junk I hear on the news every night, I might as well stay home. I come here to get *away* from that stuff."

I've learned that political operatives must be dealt with firmly. It is imperative to have an honest conversation about why political activism in the church is harmful. But be prepared: It might take a while to finally get through to them. Highly political people are known for being hard-headed and relentless. As I learned with the flyers that mysteriously appeared at the Welcome Center, even when they know what they're *not* supposed to do, they will quietly try to put something over on you. If they were only as committed to promoting Jesus as they are their favorite political candidates!

That is the struggle of ministry, though, isn't it? It's all about trying to get people to set their eyes on the things above (Col. 3:1–3).

#11

THE CONSPIRACY THEORIST

Of all the troublesome people on this list, the conspiracy theorist may be the most confounding. When I have encountered them, I have often been left speechless, without a clue as to how to respond to their anger. A conspiracy theorist believes that nothing happens by accident—that there is evil intent in every unfortunate incident that occurs.

Take the odd case of a man I will call Melvin. For several years, he'd been a member in good standing of the church I was serving. He wasn't extremely involved, but he was at church every Sunday and was friendly. We were not close, but we smiled and shook hands and exchanged a little small talk whenever our paths crossed. As far as I was concerned, we had a good relationship, though not a deep one.

One Wednesday evening, I was leading a prayer time before our adult Bible study. Someone mentioned that Melvin had been in the hospital for a few days. I was unaware. Neither Melvin nor his wife (nor anyone else) had called to tell me, so I finished leading the Bible study and then went straight to the hospital. It was out of my way and it was getting late; but I had a full schedule the following day, so I decided to go see him right then.

Melvin was sitting up in bed when I walked into his room at about 8:45 p.m. When he saw me come through the door, he turned away and looked out the window. He didn't smile or say hi or in any way acknowledge me. When I greeted him, he acted as if he didn't hear me. Puzzled, I said hello a second time and got the same response. Sometimes I can be a little slow, but in this case, I figured out right away that something was wrong. Here's how our conversation went:

> Me: Melvin, what's wrong? Why won't you look at me or speak to me?
>
> Melvin (turning slowly to look at me): This is my third day here, and you haven't been in to see me.
>
> Me: I just found out you were here a little over an hour ago. Someone mentioned it at Bible study. We prayed for you, and I decided to stop by and see you on my way home.
>
> Melvin: I've been a member of that church for years. You'd think I could get a visit from the preacher.
>
> Me: You're *getting* a visit from the preacher right now. I'm here. I came as soon as I could after finding out you were here.
>
> Melvin: I've been wondering what you were trying to tell me by not coming to see me.

I stood by his bed, completely flummoxed. I've made a million mistakes in my life and ministry; but in this case, I had done absolutely nothing wrong. If anything, I had gone a little above the call of duty by driving out of my way to go see him at almost nine o'clock at night. It had been a long day and I was tired, yet there I was. It didn't matter. He was completely convinced that I was up to something nefarious, that I was trying to tell him something. What could it possibly have been? That I didn't like him, even though all I'd ever done was be nice to him? None of it made any sense, but he was convinced that something dastardly was going on.

The crazy thing is that Melvin and his wife never came back to our church. They also told all of their friends how I had disrespected him. I made one attempt to restore our relationship but was completely rebuffed. It still stands out as one of the weirdest encounters with a church member I've ever had.

Another incident also comes to mind when I think about conspiracy theorists.

I'll call him Pete. Again, he was a nice guy who was at church every Sunday. We had a pleasant enough relationship, so I never would have guessed we'd have a problem. Then one Sunday morning, he walked up to me and stuck out his hand. Though I had shaken his hand a hundred times before, on that day I pulled my hand back and said, "I better not today, Pete, I have a cold." I did. If I hadn't had to preach, I wouldn't even have been at church. Pete gave me a surprised look and said, "You won't shake my hand?" I repeated that I had a cold and didn't want to give him my germs. "Are you trying to tell me something?" he responded. "Do you not want me to come to church here?" Honestly, his comment was so surprising that I thought he was pulling my leg, so I chuckled. Bad move. It turned out he wasn't pulling my leg and my chuckle lit a fire in him. He never came back to our church after that day—in fact, he told people that he wasn't wanted in our church.

I'll say it again: I do not understand these people.

They think everything is a conspiracy directed against them, that there are hidden meanings and cryptic messages in everything that happens. Even when there's no history to support such a notion and they can't articulate any sensible reason for a conspiracy, they still believe there is one.

I do understand this, though: Such people can do the church a lot of damage. Not just because they tell their story, but because they embellish their story. In both of the examples I just shared, I believe I was completely without fault, but the men involved made me sound like a terrible person as they told their stories around the community.

Obviously, when something hurtful happens to one of your members and you as a church leader are at fault, you need to own it and apologize. Do whatever you can to patch things up. But when you're *not* at fault and someone insists on portraying you as the devil anyway, I recommend you take it as a clear sign that there's no reason to carry on the relationship. Yes, I'm saying that if the person wants leave, let him go. Don't try to talk him into staying. And don't look at it as a failure, but as a step toward building a healthier church; because if the person will trash you when you haven't done anything wrong, imagine how he might react when you *do* make a mistake.

I realize there are people who believe you should never give up on someone—that even when you're pushed away, you should keep trying to make a connection because all things are possible with God. You just never know when God might cause a breakthrough to happen. Yet, I also remember that Jesus told his disciples to shake the dust off of their sandals and move on when they weren't well received (Matt. 10:14). I'm all for going the extra mile with people, but a conspiracy theorist is exceptionally difficult because he doesn't deal in reality. How do you reason with someone who believes in things that are not real? I think of those who are convinced that the government is hiding evidence of UFOs. In their minds, every denial only makes the government a bigger liar.

It's sad to say, but in church ministry you occasionally run into people with whom you just can't work. A conspiracy theorist, who has convinced himself that you are out to get him, is a good example. You'll be happier and accomplish much more in ministry if you release such people and focus on those who *don't* believe you're spending all your free time plotting ways to injure them.

#10

THE ONE-DAY WONDER

For too many people, being a Christian is a one-day-a-week proposition. They walk into the church building on Sunday morning well dressed, smiling, and greeting friends. They sing the songs, take Communion, and listen to the sermon. They might even compliment the preacher on a job well done before they go someplace nice for lunch with friends, praying before the meal. The problem is that when they get home and hang those church clothes in the closet, they also put away their Christian demeanor.

Though it was many years ago, I'll never forget the day I met with a group of people concerning a project we had going at church. It was a blistering hot day, and the air conditioning wasn't working. One of the women helping with the project was wearing long sleeves and a high collar. She looked like she was about to melt from the heat, so I made a comment about her long sleeves—something to the effect that I was sure she would have chosen something else if she'd known the air conditioning was going to be out. A few minutes later, another woman in the group caught me alone and said, "Please don't say anything more about her long sleeves." I was confused. What I'd said didn't seem inappropriate in any way. When I asked what was wrong with my comment, she told me that the woman was wearing long sleeves to hide bruises.

The realization of what she was telling me felt like a gut punch. I knew her husband and considered him a friend. He was in church every Sunday. I never dreamed he would be the type to physically abuse his wife. Clearly, he was a different guy throughout the week than he was on Sunday. Later, I spoke to the abused woman and offered to speak to her husband. Although she was grateful for my concern and support, she pleaded with me not to talk to him out of fear of what he might do to her afterward. She assured me she was working on a solution. It was a problem I literally lost sleep over, but I respected her wishes. It wasn't long before they separated.

On another occasion, I walked into a hardware store less than a mile from our church building. I'd been in there enough times that the proprietor knew me, though I wouldn't say we were friends. As soon as he saw me, he said, "Aha! Just the guy I want to see!" Jokingly, I said, "Oh no, sounds like I'm in trouble."

The store owner asked me if I knew a certain man and if he attended our church. Immediately, I sensed that what I was about to hear was not going to be good. When I acknowledged that the man did indeed attend our church, the store owner said, "Well, you should have been here fifteen minutes ago. He was standing right where you are shouting curses at us." My heart sank. He went on to explain the dispute they'd had. I wasn't sure who was right or wrong with regard to the dispute, but I knew the church member shouldn't have been shouting curses. I told the owner that I was very sorry the incident had happened, that we would never condone such behavior at our church. His face held a bit of a smirk as I completed my transaction and walked out the door feeling depressed.

Say hello to the one-day wonder, the church member who acts like a model Christian one day a week. I believe there are more of these people in our churches than we realize. It usually takes some bizarre incident like the ones I just described for us to realize who they are, because we generally only see them on the day they're behaving. It's always a crushing blow. You think you know someone, and then you realize you don't.

If you've looked at the table of contents of this book, then you know there's a chapter coming about the hypocrite. You may be thinking that the one-day wonder *is* a hypocrite, and you wouldn't be wrong. But I believe a lot of one-day wonders are more clueless than they are hypocritical. They just don't get it. Somehow, they haven't figured out that Christianity is more than just a Sunday exercise. They actually see themselves as fulfilling their Christian duty when they go to church. They check the box, and then they move on to the rest of their week—with no idea how much damage they do.

Right now, there are countless pastors wondering why their churches don't seem to be going anywhere. They've worked hard to build a solid program. They put their all into their preaching and pastoral work. They feel like they have committed people in their church. Still, things seem flat. Nothing is happening. A few visitors trickle in, but not many. In such situations, I often shudder to think how many one-day wonders are out in the community, giving the church a bad name. Although that's something you can never really know for sure, it would explain a lack of fervor for the church in the community, especially if it's a smaller community where people know each other well and word gets around.

In Acts 2, the early church put forth an exceptional witness and enjoyed the good will of the people in the community as a result. Then, the very next line says that people were being added to the church day by day (v. 38). There is an undeniable connection between the way people in the community view the church and the church's growth. And the way people in the community view the church is going to have a lot to do with how the members of that church conduct themselves—not just on Sunday but also during the week. I wish more church members understood how little it takes to leave a bad taste in people's mouths.

This truth was impressed on me one weekend when my wife and I were on vacation, and we visited the church of one of the most famous pastors in America. I'm confident that every person who reads this book would recognize his name—he's that famous. We were excited to attend the service and left feeling blessed. However, as we were walking toward the parking lot, we were a couple of paces behind another group of churchgoers who were talking loudly enough for us to hear. Their conversation was peppered with profanity, which would have been shocking on any Sunday, but was even more shocking on that day because the sermon we'd just heard was on the importance of controlling the tongue!

Sadly, when I think of the day we visited that church, this incident always comes to mind. I wish it didn't, but it does. Obviously, I don't blame the pastor any more than I blame myself for the curses my own church member used in the hardware store. But it's amazing how that moment raises its hand and waves every time I think of that church. I wouldn't be surprised if the hardware store owner also thinks of the cussing out he got every time he hears our church name mentioned.

It's impossible to put into words how counterproductive this is to the cause of Christ. I said earlier that when my brothers and I were young, my mom would get frustrated by how quickly the house got messed up again after she had cleaned and straightened it. She said, "It's like you boys follow me around undoing everything I do!" A pastor could say the same thing about the one-day wonder. You preach a heartfelt sermon on Sunday, and he goes out on Monday and turns it on its head.

I've often thought that it's probably a good thing we usually don't know when the people in our churches fail to put forth a good witness. It might drive us crazy if we did. I resigned myself to the fact that I couldn't make people behave, nor could I confront everybody I heard about who put forth a lousy witness. The best any of us can do is keep preaching our hearts out, pleading with people to say and do God-honoring things at all times.

#9

THE BLABBERMOUTH

Discretion is critical in church work. If you're in leadership, then you're going to learn things about your church members that are extremely personal and sensitive. Things that could destroy their livelihoods and reputations if they were known. There are a few reasons for this.

For one, *many people lived very differently before they accepted Christ.* Churches are filled with people who, at one time, were criminals and reprobates. In fact, I can say without hesitation that the power of God to change lives was my greatest source of inspiration as a pastor. I have been bowled over by some of the stories my own church members have told me about their lives before Christ. I once had a nice elderly lady tell me that she was a gunrunner for a well-known gangster during Prohibition. She said she would load up her car trunk with pistols and machine guns and drive them to wherever the next bank robbery was going to be. They had her do it because she was a sweet-looking young girl the cops wouldn't look at twice.

Also, *people become very good at hiding, and sometimes their cover is blown.* One day I got a phone call from a woman who was hysterical. She told me the police just showed up at her house out of the blue, handcuffed her husband, and drove him away. This was a man who was an active member of our church, so I was equally shocked. It turned out that he'd been married previously and had a child none of us knew about. He was years behind on child support payments, and the law finally caught up with him.

Finally, *the process of counseling someone through a problem will often expose unbecoming information.* You sit down to talk to a couple about their rocky marriage, thinking you're going to have a conversation about communication breakdowns or overspending; and the next thing you know, you're having a conversation about an affair or a pornography addiction or a drinking problem. I learned early on in my ministry that counseling appointments can produce hairpin turns that take you places you never dreamed you would go.

Many years ago, the church I was serving hired a new church secretary. She had quite an excellent employment history, but she'd never been a church secretary before. During the interview process, I warned her that in the course of doing her job she could possibly learn some things about people that might surprise or disappoint her, and that she would need to absolutely respect their privacy and keep her mouth shut. A few months into her employment, she told me that the most difficult adjustment she had to make in her job was knowing things about people she wished she didn't know.

The vast majority of church leaders with whom I have worked have been exemplary in their commitment to keeping private things private. Unfortunately, all it takes is one blabbermouth to cause deep hurt and embarrassment and drive someone right out of the church. I recall the time our leadership team discussed something highly sensitive in a meeting. It was one of those this-doesn't-leave-this-room conversations. The following week, someone—who had not been in that room—walked up to me in the lobby and asked me about it. I knew instantly that we had a blabbermouth on our leadership team. We quickly assembled the team and went around the room, demanding to know who had blabbed. Unsurprisingly, one of our new leaders confessed.

The book of James says that the tongue is a little thing that causes big problems. The author compares it to a spark that sets an entire forest on fire (3:5–6). He's right. I've seen it happen, which is why I put the blabbermouth in the top ten most troublesome church members. Thankfully, though the blabbermouth is a top ten troublemaker, the fix is pretty simple—and no, I'm not talking about duct-taping the person's mouth shut (though I've seen a few situations where I was tempted to do that!).

First, *the leadership team simply must police itself.* They are the people who know the most sensitive information, and therefore have the potential to do the most damage if they flap their gums. In my opinion, it should be two strikes and you're out. Everybody deserves a second chance, but if the person violates a confidence a second time, then he or she obviously doesn't understand—or care about—what's at stake. It's always hard to remove a church leader, but sometimes you find out you made a mistake by promoting someone to a position of leadership. Seeing the mistake and doing nothing about it invites trouble. And trouble has never been known to turn down an invitation.

Second, *blabbermouths who are not in leadership need to be confronted.* I've focused on church leaders in this chapter because that is where a lot of sensitive information ends up. But nonleaders can do a lot of damage too. In my experience, a lot of the blabbing they do falls under the heading of rumor-mongering:

- "Her husband never gets home until late at night. It's like he doesn't want to come home or something. Their marriage must not be good."
- "How can he possibly afford to drive a vehicle like that on his salary? Where is he getting that extra money?"
- "I saw her at the supermarket, and she was in the liquor aisle for ten minutes. I had no idea they were such drinkers."

It's simply impossible to build a healthy culture in your church if you allow people to run their mouths irresponsibly. If you allow them to gossip and spread rumors and criticize without restraint, then the whole atmosphere of your church will be poisoned and people will leave. I'm not suggesting you practice Gestapo-like tactics to keep people in line. But clearly, when someone is known to have said something hurtful or untrue, he or she should be approached. It can be done discreetly and kindly. It can also be a teaching opportunity. If the person reacts angrily and chooses to leave the church, rest easy. In all likelihood, the culture and quality of life in your church will have just improved.

During World War II, Seagram's Distillers published a poster designed by Seymour Goff. It showed a ship on fire and sinking into the ocean and featured the words, "Loose lips might sink ships." The poster was designed to be hung in bars and taverns across America to remind citizens that spies were in the country and that loose talk could undermine the war effort and get people killed. While I don't advocate for hanging similar posters in our church buildings, wise leaders know that loose lips are dangerous and must be taken seriously if the church is to be strong and healthy.

PART THREE

THE DEADLY

Satan directs immense efforts at subverting Christian communities. He knows that lone individuals pose little threat to his kingdom. They are also easy prey that he can dispatch at his leisure. Only the body of Christ worries Satan enough to draw his best efforts, and when Satan gives his best, that's bad news for the people of God![14]

Dennis McCallum, *Satan and His Kingdom*

#8

THE LOTHARIO

In the early 1600s, Miguel de Cervantes wrote *Don Quixote*, which some people believe is the best novel ever written. In one scene, the protagonist becomes obsessed with testing his wife's marital faithfulness, so he talks his close friend, Lothario, into trying to seduce her. From there, the word *lothario* gradually came to be used to refer to a playboy who tries to seduce women. I am using it in that sense here, though I am certainly not suggesting that only men indulge in the art of seduction. There are plenty of female lotharios.

Proven Men, an organization that helps men in their quest to be sexually pure, conducted a survey in conjunction with the Barna Group that indicated that 35 percent of married men and 17 percent of married women are having affairs. Even more disheartening is the fact that infidelity is impacting Christian marriages at the same rate.[15] We want to believe that Christians are better at remaining pure than unbelievers. It just seems like that would *have* to be the case. But if the surveys are to be believed, then it isn't. In fact, if you *really* want to feel discouraged, consider the well-publicized stat that 33 percent of pastors admit to having had an affair.

Of course, sexual impurity among God's people is nothing new. Samson was Hugh Hefner in a loincloth, David's affair with Bathsheba stands as one of the most uncomfortable stories in the Bible, and David's son, Solomon, somehow ended up with more wives than there are players in the entire NBA. Things didn't get much better in the New Testament. When Paul wrote to the Corinthians, he expressed shock at their sexual permissiveness, suggesting they were even worse in this regard than pagans (1 Cor. 5:1).

Every Christian who has an affair has his or her own unique story. I'd like to believe that most are not looking for an illicit sexual relationship, but rather find themselves slipping into one for reasons that have little to do with sex. There are, however, people who are on the prowl and who see the church as a happy hunting ground. There are always single people who feel lonely, and even some of those who are married may be unhappy. Plus, lots of planned social activities create opportunities to mingle. Jon Acuff, author of *Stuff Christians Like*, talks about seeing a copy of *Details* (a now defunct men's magazine) that carried the headline: "The Hottest Pickup Spot in Hollywood . . . Is a Church."[16]

Quite a few years ago, a man who was a young leader in our church came to see me, looking troubled. "I think I've got a problem," he said. "And I don't know what to do." He then told me that a young woman in our church was calling him multiple times a day. They'd worked on a ministry project together and had become acquainted. He said that more than once a day she would call with a super-cheerful voice just to see what he was up to or to share something funny that had happened to her since the last time she called. She hadn't said anything sexually provocative, but the number of calls, the lack of a reason for calling, and the fact that he was married made the situation wildly inappropriate. He'd asked her not to call, suggesting that people (including his wife) might get the wrong idea, but she blew off his concerns as if they were silly and refused to back off.

Here's how I knew she was a female lothario: After he asked her several times not to call and got no cooperation, I spoke with her at his request. When I echoed his concerns about appearances and suggested her calls were inappropriate given his marital status and his repeated requests for her to stop calling, she blew up, denying at the top of her lungs that she was doing anything wrong. My secretary in the adjacent office heard her screaming at me and almost dialed 911. I couldn't help thinking of Queen Gertrude's line in

Hamlet: "The lady doth protest too much, methinks." She reacted the way one does when a nerve is hit.

I admired the man for coming to me with his problem. If he'd been less concerned about his purity and his marriage, he might have been inclined to play along with the little game the woman was obviously trying to get started. If that had happened, there's little doubt something illicit would have developed. That, in turn, could have led to the end of a marriage, a church scandal, and serious collateral damage. Who knows how many people, especially those who looked up to him, might have had their faith seriously damaged by his moral failure? And how many skeptics would have had a field day ridiculing Christians and claiming we're all hypocrites? This is why I listed the lothario in the "deadly" category. We are now into territory where the stakes are higher and the potential for damage is much greater.

Allow me to suggest three reasons why affairs happen in churches.

First, *there are more than a few people in church involved in difficult marriages*. That's counterintuitive, isn't it? It's easy to assume that people who come to church are all just happy little Jesus followers. But the truth is, the very reason countless people come to church in the first place is because they're unhappy and looking for help or hope—and for many, that unhappiness is centered in their marriage. You can ask any pastor. There seems to be a never-ending parade of people looking for marriage counseling. When I was a pastor, I had to start referring couples to a Christian counselor in our city because I simply didn't have time to handle the load.

Second, at church, *an unhappily married person is likely to meet someone friendly and kind, who at least gives the impression of being a good person*. It's not like going to a bar, where desperation hangs in the air like fog, and you can see when people are drinking heavily and trying to pick up someone. When you meet someone at church, you automatically assume the person has moral values, that he or she is in church because there's at least some concern about being right with God. For an unhappily married person whose spouse is uninterested in spiritual things, meeting someone friendly and nice at church can feel refreshing.

Third, *the wholesome church environment makes it easy for people to delude themselves into believing their flirtations are harmless.* In a bar, there's no such thing as an innocent flirtation. People are on the prowl and make no bones about it. In church, there is an assumption that nobody is on the prowl, so flirty comments and smiles and eye contact and light touches on the arm can be easily dismissed as insignificant. They're not insignificant. In fact, virtually every Christian I've ever talked to who had an affair told me that it started just that way: with comments, smiles, eye contact, and touches rationalized as no big deal.

Imagine a lothario stepping into this environment. Things are set up perfectly for him or her to mix and mingle and meet someone attractive and interesting. If the church has an active singles ministry, then the opportunity could be even greater.

In my experience, the lothario is not someone who immediately strikes you as trouble. Someone who is skilled in the art of seduction is, of necessity, polished and smooth. He knows what he has that works on the opposite sex—whether it's a killer smile, a sense of humor, or an "aw shucks" demeanor. And if it's a woman, you can be sure she knows how to turn on the charm too. She knows very well if the sideways glance, the flip of the hair, or the batting of eyelashes get results. Of course, there's nothing wrong with being friendly or funny or charming. Many non-lotharios are genuinely that way.

The best church leaders can do is keep an eye open for anything that seems a little off: two people who are not married to each other spending an inordinate amount of time together, someone's personality becoming much more bubbly when they're around a specific individual, or a church member suddenly becoming super-interested in serving on a ministry team that just happens to be led by a person he or she has been talking to a lot. While I'm not sure it's true 100 percent of the time, I would say that in the vast majority of cases, whenever an affair happens in church, there were red flags leading up to it. People have a hard time hiding it when that kind of attraction kicks in.

I recommend that leaders be observant and proactive if something seems amiss. It's easy to tell ourselves that people's private lives are none of our business, that we need to trust them to do the right thing and not be the Gestapo. But every single time a sex scandal explodes in a church, amid all the smoking rubble, those in leadership find themselves looking back with regret, wishing they'd paid more attention or hadn't been so quick to blow off that behavior that carried a whiff of inappropriateness.

In Romans 12:17, Paul says, "Do things in such a way that everyone can see you are honorable." This is the verse to remind people of when their behavior causes concern. They don't have to be accused of anything or made to feel like a criminal. It will likely be enough just to point out your concern about how things look. If the person responds humbly and apologetically and immediately makes changes, then you have succeeded. If the person blows up and overreacts, then you have also succeeded. You have hit a nerve, which tells you there really was something brewing.

#7

THE PHARISEE

I was a preacher for forty-six years, and I honestly don't know what I would have done without the Pharisees we meet in the Gospels. Their words and actions (and Jesus' scuffles with them) provided me with mountains of sermon ideas and illustrations galore. Anytime I needed a good example of how religious people should *not* behave, I could count on the Pharisees to provide one on a silver platter.

I quickly learned, however, that Pharisees are much more tolerable on the written page than they are in real life. When a pharisaical person shows up in your church, you're going to have headaches, hurt feelings, and probably some casualties. In Scripture, there are four qualities in particular for which Pharisees are known that make them bad news for any church today.

First, *the Pharisees were self-righteous*. They simply thought they were better than everybody else. Jesus talked about one Pharisee who prayed, "God, I thank you that I am not like other people" (Luke 18:11). This religious leader wasn't referring to having different political views or interests or hobbies. He was referring to himself as living on an entirely different plane, being more knowledgeable, more spiritual, more connected to God.

Second, *the Pharisees were extremely judgmental*. They were so into judging people that they actually went around trying to catch people in some egregious sin so they could make a big to-do about it. A case in point would be the woman caught in adultery (John 8:1–11). Typically, when people commit acts that could get them executed (and, yes, adultery was a capital offense at that time), they go to great lengths to keep their actions a secret. But somehow the Pharisees caught her in the act. Did they set a trap for her? Did they know she was attracted to a certain man and decided to follow her wherever she went until they caught her? And how did they get an eyewitness? Was someone hiding in the bedroom closet, or did someone burst through the door at just the right moment? And where was the guy? Why didn't they frog-march him out of the room too? Such questions are almost too creepy to contemplate, but they were perfectly in character for the Pharisees.

Third, *the Pharisees were notoriously closed-minded.* The main reason they rejected Jesus was because he didn't fit the reinforced concrete structure of their theology. They were expecting someone like themselves, but Jesus showed up looking and acting like a servant. They were expecting a fire-breathing politician who would take on Rome, but Jesus showed up caring a whole lot more about ordinary people than about overthrowing Rome. Even in spite of all the miracles Jesus did, which attested so clearly to his messiahship, the Pharisees rejected him because he just didn't fit their preconceived theological notions. Their minds were closed up tight. The door was nailed shut and barricaded.

Fourth, *the Pharisees were plotters and schemers.* To me, this was one of their worst qualities. They staked out their position of being opposed to Jesus. Fine. Everybody has a right to choose on which side of the Jesus question they want to be. But when it became obvious that they were wrong, when Jesus came out of the tomb alive and well, they didn't admit their error and humble themselves. They didn't make any attempt to step over to the right side of history. Rather, they launched a cover-up, a conspiracy that was as silly as it was futile.

If you take these four qualities and put them into a single person, then you've got someone who is going to be a real problem in your church.

When I was very young in ministry, I met a leader in the church I was serving who made me feel uncomfortable. I didn't have even a shadow of the knowledge about these matters that I possess now; I only knew there was something about this man that made me uneasy. He was the dominant personality, the alpha dog among all our leaders. Nothing happened in our church without his approval. And he was the type who couldn't just walk into church on Sunday morning; he had to make a grand entrance. He carried a fifteen-pound Bible, shook every hand, and could be heard over all the other voices in the room. A lot of people catered to this man—and he obviously loved it.

One weekday at dawn, I was fishing in a farm pond not far from his house, when suddenly I sensed I wasn't alone. I felt like I was being watched. As I continued to cast my lure and crank my reel, I turned my body right and left so I could look around without turning my head. Sure enough, I spotted this man in the trees, watching me. I didn't let on that I had seen him. I assumed that any minute he would come walking down the hill and say good morning, but he never did. He watched for quite a long time and then left quietly. I'm confident he never knew I was aware of his presence. I assume he saw my car go past his house and turn into the lane that led to the pond. But why did he creep into the trees and spy on me? What was there to see? It was weird.

A year or so later, that same man was instrumental in getting me fired from that church. One Sunday, I preached a sermon that didn't sit well with him. He saw the sermon as a personal attack and started a campaign to get rid of me. What's interesting is that the sermon was a simple recounting of some of the notes I had taken in my "Life of Christ" class at Bible college that very week. The topic was—you guessed it—hypocrisy. His belief that I aimed the sermon at him was ridiculous. I was so young and green (twenty years old), I wouldn't have been capable of aiming a sermon at anybody. Somehow, he took the sermon personally and, in typical Pharisee fashion, judged me harshly and set in motion a plot to get rid of me.

One night, a good friend of mine in the church called me. He let me know that this man was calling key church members, telling them I had committed insubordination, and asking for their support in having me removed at a special board meeting. I feel pretty confident that the people sensed injustice, because several members mentioned to me that they felt bad about what was happening. No one, however, had the courage to stand up to the man calling the shots.

Yes, if you've got a Pharisee in your church, you've got trouble—real trouble if you've got more than one.

So what do you do?

I believe the confrontations Jesus had with the Pharisees were included in Scripture to help us understand how we should deal with them today. Consider some of the things Jesus did that we can do.

First, *Jesus identified them*. Boy, did he identify them! He identified them with words so strong, they almost make us squirm. He called them blind guides, fools, serpents, vipers, hypocrites, and whitewashed tombs. I was raised on the notion that I shouldn't call people names, and you probably were too. This probably includes Jesus as well! That he made an exception with the Pharisees tells you how bad they were. He wanted to call them out in a way that would leave no doubt they were the bad guys.

I find this incredibly refreshing, because today we seem to be scared to death to call troublemakers what they are. We're more likely to make excuses for them, to talk about how they may be difficult but they have other good qualities. Or how they're difficult, but they mean well. Or they're difficult, but that's just their personality type. If, like me, you've ever wondered how troublemakers are able to afflict a church for decades without ever being called out, this is how it happens. Jesus would never have engaged in such tip-toeing.

Let me be clear: I am not advocating for calling these people snakes or fools. I *am* advocating for identifying them for what they are and not making excuses for them.

Second, *Jesus was specific in pointing out their sin.* He understood that ambiguity doesn't cut it when you're dealing with a problem. For example, saying there's a problem in the back of the house is not nearly as helpful as saying the master bathroom sink is clogged. So Jesus didn't just say the Pharisees were a problem or a headache or a source of frustration. He said, "They crush people with unbearable religious demands and never lift a finger to ease the burden" (Matt. 23:4). He also said, directly to them, "You are careful to tithe even the tiniest income from your herb gardens, but you ignore the more important aspects of the law—justice, mercy, and faith" (Matt. 23:23). Again and again, he spelled out exactly what they were doing that hindered the purposes of God.

Likewise, we must be specific when dealing with troublemakers. I've seen too many cases where church trouble centered on people's feelings about each other rather than the actual sin that had been committed. When feelings are at the center of things, you're going to have an escalation of the situation, guaranteed. By setting feelings aside and focusing on the actual offense, we keep the way clear to make progress.

Third, *Jesus refused to negotiate with the Pharisees.* They held completely opposite positions on many issues, but Jesus didn't offer to meet them in the middle. He never said, "Let's sit down and talk over this situation. Surely, we can work something out that is mutually agreeable." Jesus knew what was right and refused to bend an inch. Compromise was not even a consideration.

In many churches today, leaders seem to think it's their job to solve problems in ways that make everybody happy. Is it because we're afraid that if we take a hard line against sin, people will leave and take some of their friends with them? Do we believe that living with a troublemaker in our midst is better than seeing our numbers shrink?

I've worked with church leaders who sincerely felt that it was their job to hang onto every church member, that a defection could only be interpreted as leadership failure. I disagree, and I think Jesus would too. Lowering your standards to placate a troublemaker makes it impossible to have a healthy church culture and emboldens the person causing the trouble. If you make allowances for bad behavior, the only thing you can be sure of is that you'll get more of it. It's far better to keep your standards high—if you lose a troublemaker and his supporters as a result, then consider it addition by subtraction.

Courage is the key to dealing with Pharisees. We see it in Jesus. While others stepped aside for them, Jesus stood up to them. We need church leaders who won't be afraid to confront the troublemaker with a strong personality. When we take away their ability to intimidate us, we negate one of their most effective weapons and gain the upper hand.

Of course, we mustn't forget that it was his opposition to the Pharisees that got Jesus killed. We need no more of a reminder than that to tell us that we could suffer some backlash too. But, like Jesus, we should see it as a price worth paying to protect the kingdom May the example of Jesus—who stood before them with his jaw set and never backed up an inch—be our inspiration.

#6

THE FALSE TEACHER

James 3:1 says, "Dear brothers and sisters, not many of you should become teachers in the church, for we who teach will be judged more strictly." There are two reasons a teacher might get a harsh judgment from God: one is teaching the gospel but not living it; the other is teaching a twisted or perverted gospel. Although both are bad, I want to address the latter here.

I've asked many people why they chose the church they attend, and they usually give one of three answers: it's close to where they live, they like the preacher (or the music or something), or a friend goes there and invited them. Much can be learned from these answers, such as the fact that not very many are thinking about doctrine when they choose a church.

I recall a family that was active in our church. They were good people who were heavily involved, but because of a job change they had to move to another city. I and many others in our church hated to see them go. After they had time to get settled into their new community, we connected and I asked if they had found a church they liked. I was stunned to hear they had chosen to attend a church that was part of a denomination well known for not believing in the inerrancy of Scripture. Apparently, it was close to their new home and had an impressive facility and lots of activities to get involved in. They said they felt blessed to have found such a "great" church.

Let's face it: church doctrine is not on many people's minds. Among members of the typical church, especially one that's growing, there's usually a cobb salad of theological opinions. Although the church may have its official doctrinal statement posted on its website, the average attender won't know or care what it says. They may never even look at it. They might shrug and say, "People are always going to argue about religion, but that stuff doesn't mean anything to me. I have my relationship with Jesus and that's all I need. As long as the church meets my family's needs, I'm happy."

While many churchgoers do not care about doctrine, *God* does. As Paul wrote to Timothy, a young preacher in Ephesus:

> Hold on to the pattern of wholesome teaching you learned from me—a pattern shaped by the faith and love that you have in Christ Jesus. Through the power of the Holy Spirit who lives within us, carefully guard the precious truth that has been entrusted to you. (2 Tim. 1:13–14)

I think we can safely assume, at the very least, that "carefully guard the precious truth" means making sure those who preach from our pulpits and teach our classes and small groups believe the Bible is inerrant and inspired by God, and that they teach it without any denominational bias or personal agenda.

Sadly, many churches aren't as diligent as they should be in this area. They're so desperate for teaching help that they'll approve anyone to teach who has a pulse and is willing. Or they'll approve some newcomer they don't really know, simply because he used to teach in his former church. Sometimes church leaders are so desperate for teaching help that they treat a new teaching volunteer the same way they treat an unexpected $500 refund that comes in the mail: just accept it and don't ask questions!

Obviously, this opens the door to false teachers.

I think most people hear the words "false teacher" and picture someone with evil intent, someone crafty and slick who's on a power trip and trying to manipulate people's minds. Although that type of person certainly does exist, in my experience, the far more common type of false teacher is the good old boy who knows just enough about the Bible to be dangerous. He's not actually trying to mislead people; he just doesn't know the Scriptures very well and ends up teaching things that aren't true. My point is that the false teacher can be a troublemaker who doesn't look or act like a troublemaker. The reason I list him at #6 on this list is not because he shows up with a tail, a pitchfork, and a plan to wreck the church, but because the mishandling of biblical truth, even if it's not done with evil intent, can bring about enormous harm.

For example, many years ago, I was on vacation and visited a well-known church. In the lobby, I struck up a conversation with one of the greeters, who was friendly and seemed eager to talk about the church. I asked a few questions about the church's beliefs, including this one: "What is the church's position on baptism?" The man said, "We don't have one. We tell people it's whatever they want to do. If they want to do it or not do it, that's fine. Or if they want to be sprinkled or immersed, it's okay. We'll do whatever they want." The man was beaming as he spoke these words. He was truly proud of his church's open-mindedness. It apparently had never occurred to him that the position on baptism he just stated was about as far from biblical as mud wrestling is from ballet. The apostle Peter did not say, "Repent, and if you'd like to be baptized that would be awesome, but don't feel obligated. We'll handle this issue any way you want." No, he said, "Repent and be baptized" (Acts 2:38).

Of course, some would say that God is all about love and would never judge someone harshly for being a little off doctrinally. Paul disagreed: "Keep a close watch on how you live and on your teaching. Stay true to what is right for the sake of your own salvation and the salvation of those who hear you" (1 Tim. 4:16).

Wait. Did he just make our teaching a salvation issue?

You bet he did.

You can tell yourself that God isn't a stickler for doctrine if you want, but you do so at your own risk. Keep in mind that there are over ninety references to doctrine or teaching in the New Testament, and all of them talk about the importance of getting it right.

Nowhere does the Bible even hint that God gives us wiggle room with regard to the key doctrines of the faith.

So, how can we keep our doctrine pure and deal with false teachers, whether evil or inept? Here are some ideas.

First, *settle the question of whether the Bible is indeed God's inspired, inerrant word.* If it isn't, then it doesn't much matter what we do with it. If it is, then it must not be tampered with or devalued by giving human opinions equal status. As you make your decision, consider that Paul himself held the Scriptures in the highest possible regard: "All Scripture is inspired by God and is useful to teach us what is true and to make us realize what is wrong in our lives" (2 Tim. 3:16). He also said, "I want you to understand that the gospel message I preach is not based on mere human reasoning. I received my message from no human source, and no one taught me. Instead, I received it by direct revelation from Jesus Christ" (Gal. 1:11–12). The passion we bring to our defense of the gospel will be determined by the way we answer this question.

Second, *lay out a strategy for recruiting and training teachers.* By filling your teaching slots with trained and qualified teachers, you virtually eliminate the possibility of someone unqualified slipping in out of desperation. So instead of sitting around and hoping that a well qualified teacher will come sauntering through the door, get busy. Identify sharp, committed people with good communication skills and a grasp of the Scriptures. Approach them. If they show an interest, then start training them. Teach them the truth so they can teach it to others.

I'd also suggest that you keep an open mind when looking for potential teachers to recruit and train. One of my favorite stories from my preaching years concerns two grandfathers who agreed to team-teach a class of fourth graders. Neither of them had never taught a class before, but they loved the Lord, saw the need, and volunteered. I never would have thought of recruiting them, but they were trustworthy guys, so we gave them some training and turned them loose. I still remember them walking through the hallways of our church with a line of happy fourth graders trailing along behind them. It was a perfect match. So, don't write someone off just because the fit seems unconventional. God works in mysterious ways.

Third, *carefully vet anyone who is a candidate to teach.* As I said, volunteers are hard to come by, especially teachers. I can understand why pastors practically hyperventilate when someone steps up and says, "I'd be happy to teach that class." If it's someone you know well or someone whom people you trust have recommended, then fine. But if not, then the person needs to be carefully vetted. Even if you're desperate, tap the brakes. It's better to put a class on hiatus until a qualified teacher can be found than to stick someone you don't know in there who may end up teaching false doctrine.

When it comes to the vetting process, I recommend that the prospective teacher be interviewed by the pastor and elders. Every attempt should be made to ensure that the person is humble and kind, has good communication skills, is dependable, has a thorough grasp of the Scriptures, and holds views compatible with the church's positions on those issues deemed nonnegotiable. If a high level of compatibility can't be established, then the person shouldn't be allowed to teach, no matter how eager he or she is—or how desperate the pastor is.

Fourth, when a problem is identified, meet it head-on. If you get wind of something questionable being taught about one of the church's nonnegotiables, then look into it. Ask questions. It could be that the teacher was misquoted. As a long-time pastor, I couldn't begin to count the number of times I was accused of saying something I didn't say. But if the report is correct and something inaccurate was indeed taught, then the elders should meet with the teacher. Without question, the discussion should be amicable, with the only agenda being to honor God. If the teacher becomes defensive or holds a position on a nonnegotiable issue the elders believe is unbiblical and incompatible with the church's beliefs, then the teacher should be asked to step down. If, however, the teacher was simply in error and is willing to accept correction, then this is a victory for the kingdom and bodes well for that person's future as a teacher.

To conclude, never forget that the Song of Songs speaks of the little foxes as being the ones that ruin the vineyard (Song 2:15). I would say the same thing about false doctrines. It's probably not the "Jesus is not the Son of God" doctrine that's going to infect our churches. We'll recognize that bad boy right off and blow him up. Rather, it's the subtle, almost unnoticeable false doctrines that ease us ever-so-gently away from the truth. For an example, think about that faithful Christian who stands by the casket of a deceased church member and says, "God must have needed another angel, so he called ole Joe home." People will likely sigh and smile and nod in agreement. But if you were holding a false doctrine detector, it would be screeching like a fire alarm.

The point is that false doctrines can surface outside the classroom too. Wise church leaders will be always on the lookout for them and face them boldly when they surface, but always with a loving spirit.

#5

THE CONTROL FREAK

When I was in high school, I worked at a furniture store after school and on Saturdays. My boss, the store owner, was one of the kindest and most wonderful men I've ever met. But there was one thing he did that I had to get used to. No matter what job he gave me to do, whether it was assembling a table or rearranging some items on the showroom floor or loading the truck for a delivery, he kept checking on me and constantly and asking questions: "Mark, wouldn't a bigger screwdriver work better?" "Did you get the right size bulb for that lamp?" "Did you tighten the screws really good?" "Did you save the extra hardware?"

This went on for the duration of my four years there, long after I had proven I could complete these tasks to his satisfaction. He didn't mean any offense; it was just his way and we even joked about it. When I walked into the showroom to place a new lamp I had assembled on an empty table—and he walked right behind me and moved it one inch (which he *always* did)—I would teasingly tell him how much better the lamp looked sitting one inch from where I had placed it. "I don't know what I was thinking when I set it where I did," I would say. He would grin and respond, "Mark, you know I can't help it."

His need to control everything was never a problem, though, because he was a wonderful man with a sweet spirit. What's scary is when you find someone with a controlling spirit who *isn't* a wonderful man or woman with a sweet spirit.

A number of years ago, a man started attending our church who seemed nice. In my ministry, I quickly learned not to put too much stock in first impressions, but all the early signs indicated he would be a blessing to our church. During his first year with us, I noticed he spent a lot of time with the staff and elders. At some point, we were all invited to his home or out to eat with him and his wife. And he could always be found chatting with one of us on Sunday.

Then, at about the one-year mark, everything went sideways.

He asked to meet with the elders, along with me and my lead associate. At that meeting, he explained to us that he had a special giftedness. He said that God had given him the gift of fixing things, of seeing what was wrong with a marriage or a business or a church, and he knew how to fix it. He then proceeded to break out a five-page list of all the things we were doing wrong as a church, along with specific steps we could take to remedy the problems. He said that during his first year with our church, he had been quietly assessing us as leaders and the decisions we had made for the church, and now he felt ready to start fixing.

Of course, the arrogance of this was breathtaking to us all. Most of us had been involved with the congregation for years. We knew the people. We knew the history. We'd been through all the ups and downs. We'd earned the people's trust. Mr. Fix It (as I will call him from here on) was a newcomer in every sense of the word. He knew nothing about our history. He'd never sat in on one of our meetings, so he knew nothing about our goals or plans. And he'd done nothing to earn our trust as a leader, much less a "fixer."

Still, mostly out of sheer curiosity, we decided to listen to what he had to say.

I'll admit that some of his assessment wasn't far off. He did indeed peg some of our weaknesses, but they were weaknesses we were already well aware of. He didn't tell us one thing we didn't already know. Where he fell flat was with his proposed solutions. Predictably, they showed no understanding of our church or the plan we had laid out for the future. Several were drastic to the point of being ridiculous, including coldly laying off a truly indispensable member of our staff to create a pool of cash that would be invested in an area of ministry we weren't currently pursuing.

As he laid out his recommendations, I was thinking two things: (1) This is the most arrogant human being I have ever met, and (2) this is a power play—this man is trying to take over our church. I and, I later learned, all the rest of our leaders felt that what was happening was not being driven by the Holy Spirit as the man claimed. That feeling was confirmed when we started pushing back against his over-the-top suggestions and he became angry. Very angry. He told us that we were naive and that God had sent him to our church to help us, implying that if we didn't bow to his "expertise" we were going against God.

The good news is that, after that meeting, Mr. Fix It never set foot in our church building again. When he saw that he wasn't going to be able to start pulling strings and make us his little marionettes, he left.

We rejoiced and considered it addition by subtraction.

Unfortunately, sometimes control freaks don't leave. Sometimes they stay and pour their energy into complaining and criticizing the leaders they feel are standing in their way. The following are actual statements frustrated control freaks have made about the church leaders they felt were shutting them out of the leadership circle:

- "I've told them what they need to do, but they won't listen."
- "They just want yes-men to agree with whatever they say."
- "They wouldn't know a good idea if it came with a marching band."
- "How could we not have problems in this church? Look who's in charge!"

Obviously, such talk is a cancer for any church. I've observed three main qualities that seem evident in most control freaks.

1. *Arrogance.* They see themselves as being smarter than everyone else. They think they see what no one else sees, understand what no one else understands, and have more brilliant ideas than anyone has ever thought of. This was the central personality trait of Mr. Fix It. Arrogance dripped from his fingertips.
2. *A possessive spirit.* I always loved it when someone came to me with a great idea for our church. Everything good in this world started with a great idea. But I quickly learned that some people are possessive of their ideas. They get testy if you don't let them be in charge and run it their way. Sometimes, they take offense if you want to modify their idea to make it better.
3. *A lack of patience.* This is one I have to watch out for in my own life. For example, if I see someone trying to do something I know I can do as well or better in half the time, I have a burning urge to step in and take over. When I was a pastor, I would often look at a job that needed to be done and say to myself, "It'll be quicker and easier for me to do it myself than to find someone to do it and show them how." Although delegating and training are vital, it takes time and patience. To paraphrase comic Jeff Foxworthy: If you find yourself doing things yourself instead of recruiting and training help, you might be a control freak.

It doesn't take much of an imagination to picture the damage an arrogant person who is possessive and refuses to share the load can do to your church. So let me offer three suggestions on how to defend against them.

First, *build a team-oriented culture.* In 1958, Leonard Read published an essay called "I, Pencil." A portion of it reads as follows:

> I am a lead pencil—the ordinary wooden pencil familiar to all boys and girls and adults who can read and write. . . . I am a mystery—

> more so than a tree or a sunset or even a flash of lightning. But, sadly, I am taken for granted by those who use me, as if I were a mere incident and without background. I have a profound lesson to teach. And I can teach this lesson better than can an automobile or an airplane or a mechanical dishwasher because—well, because I am seemingly so simple. Simple? Yet, not a single person on the face of this earth knows how to make me.[17]

Could it be true that no one on earth knows how to make a pencil?

Actually, yes. Because a pencil is made of so many things: wood, lead, metal, lacquer, ink for the labeling, and an eraser. No one person handles all of these steps in a pencil's construction. Pencils are made by teams—and so are most other great things, including churches.

This, of course, is biblical. Jesus chose twelve disciples. Later, when those men were leading the infant church, they were careful not to allow power to become centralized in one person. In Acts 6, when there was a failure in the distribution of food, they didn't choose one man to be in charge of fixing it; they chose seven. The Bible also teaches a plurality of elders (Titus 1:5). Again and again in Scripture, we see teams functioning effectively in the Lord's service, reaching the lost, and growing the church. And so it should be in the modern church.

One of the best ways to protect your church from the control freak is to create an expectation that things will be done together, through teamwork and cooperation. I'm happy to say that when Mr. Fix It started working through his five pages of criticisms and fixes for our church, I knew exactly what was going through my coleaders' heads. They were thinking: "Nope. This is not how we do things around here. You don't get to come in here and start telling everybody what to do." Mr. Fix It didn't know it, but his boat had sprung a leak before he even got to page two. In fact, he wasn't able to finish his presentation before he was shut down. I believe the reason he left after that meeting and never returned to our church is because he could see that our team-oriented culture refused to accommodate his desire to be the Top Dog.

Second, *be slow to plug people in as leaders.* In 1 Timothy 3, Paul gave strict qualifications. He also instructed the church in Ephesus to allow time for people to be tested before they were allowed to serve as deacons (1 Tim. 3:10). This is wise, because potential troublemakers generally reveal their true colors before too long. It took our Mr. Fix It a year, which is longer than most control freaks. They're usually champing at the bit long before that. Show me a church where it's easy to become a leader, and I'll show you a church that has leadership problems.

Third, *shut down any power play immediately.* The moment you observe someone getting a little too big for his britches, step in. If you wait, he will expand his base and tighten his grip. A good example from the Bible is Absalom, David's son, who made a power play for the ages. Read in 2 Samuel 15 and see how he went around wooing people to support him in a revolt against his father. People obsessed with control always try to woo those they think can help expand their power base.

Sometimes, church leaders are too slow to pick up on this and respond. They think they're looking at a guy who's bubbling over with passion, when they're really looking at a guy who's obsessed. They think they're watching a guy work hard for the Lord ,when he's really working hard for himself. By the time they realize they've misread the individual, damage has often already been done.

One red flag that will help you avoid misreading people is to be suspicious of flowery speech. When Mr. Fix It presented his criticisms and recommendations to our leaders, he dressed them up in spiritual language, telling us how much he had prayed and how much God had led him and inspired him and how deeply he cared about our church. We were supposed to hear those hot-button spiritual words and roll over, but our team-oriented mindset wouldn't allow it. When we started expressing concerns and asking hard questions, all that flowery spirituality he supposedly brought into the room with him suddenly disappeared. Almost immediately, he got testy when he sensed things weren't going to go his way. Don't let the control freak's "spiritual act" fool you. Anytime you see someone trying to take control, shut him down.

I heard something in a sermon many years ago that has always stuck with me, which pretty well sums up the control freak: "You'll notice that the person who tries so hard to change you will not be the slightest bit interested in changing himself."

#4

THE SNOB

A snob is a person who thinks they're above you. They observe that you aren't as educated as they are, or don't dress as well as they do, or don't live in as nice a house or neighborhood or aren't as spiritual, and therefore they conclude that you are beneath them. The snob is haughty and aloof when they're with people they feel aren't their equal. They're offended by much of what others say and do and criticize them mercilessly. The snob is one of the most unpleasant people on earth.

Snobbery has been around a long time and many of us tend to accept it as normal. Throughout history, we've always judged people by their clothing, manners, and cultural tastes. Language and dialect are especially revealing. You speak one way if you're of the so-called upper class and another way if you're of the lower. In 1913, Irish playwright George Bernard Shaw wrote *Pygmalion*, which later evolved into the musical *My Fair Lady*. It was all about a cockney flower girl who took lessons in phonetics from a professor so she could be a lady. Little has changed today.

American pop culture is loaded with striking pictures of snobbishness. My favorite movie, *The Wizard of Oz*, features the snooty, bicycle-peddling grouch, Almira Gulch, who might be the snobbiest character in movie history. Think also about how many movies there are that show snobbishness among teens. Even Dr. Seuss dabbled in snobbery with his story "The Sneetches," about strange yellow creatures who feel superior or inferior to each other depending on whether they have a star on their bellies.

You can find snobbery even in the New Testament. Remember when Philip told Nathanael that he had found the Messiah, a man from Nazareth named Jesus? Nathanael's response had more than a tinge of snobbishness in it: "Can anything good come from Nazareth?" (John 1:46). And who could forget the nameless but famous Pharisee who loudly thanked the Lord that he was not like other people (Luke 18:11)?

If you talk to people who have quit the church, you'll learn that many of them dropped out because they didn't feel welcome or accepted. I remember one woman describing her family's experience in a church they had just left. "We worshiped there for a year," she said, "but were never able to break through the bubble. We always felt like outsiders." I also recall numerous instances when someone would call me with questions about our church. It was common to hear someone ask, "Do people at your church dress up?" I knew that question was code for: "If I don't wear fancy clothes, am I going to be accepted?" Clearly, the person had run into some religious snobs at some point.

Here's a sad reality: It doesn't take many snobs to hurt your church's reputation in the community. You might think that if you had one hundred sweet, loving people for every one snob, then you would have nothing to worry about. After all, that's a snob ratio of only 1 percent. But all it takes is one encounter with a haughty person to convince a visiting family that they're in the wrong church. There's an old saying that a chain is only as strong as its weakest link. Something akin to that is true of churches. Like it or not, in the eyes of visitors, your church will only be as friendly as the unfriendliest member they happen to meet. Their reality will be based on their experience, not on your belief that your church is made up of mostly wonderful people.

But snobbishness hurts the church in other ways besides just scaring away seekers. There is a kind of snobbishness that can thrive inside the congregation that divides the body of Christ.

Think about the older couple, who have grown children, observing a young couple having trouble corralling their spirited kids. The older ones shake their heads and say with an air of superiority, "*Our* kids were never allowed to do that!"

Or what about the person who attends the midweek Bible study like clockwork, carrying a thick Bible? He shakes his head in dismay when he thinks about those "worldly" church members who go to church only on Sunday morning. "I don't understand why they don't hunger and thirst for the word like I do," he says with a shake of his head.

We've all met the person who's never watched anything stronger than a Disney princess movie and is mighty proud of it. When she hears a church member mention that he recently saw the latest R-rated blockbuster, she's horrified. "I don't know how you can call yourself a Christian if you watch movies like *that*."

You've probably also met the person who is proudly nondenominational. He's more suspicious of Methodists and Baptists and Presbyterians than he is of a masked man walking into a bank holding a gun. "Well, you know how those people are," he says. "They're more loyal to their denomination than they are to Jesus."

But the most irritating church snob of all might be the person who's had a largely happy and peaceful life, yet he clucks his tongue and shakes his head at that church member who always seems embroiled in some sort of major problem. "Well, you know, God doesn't bless people who have sin in their lives. I wonder," he says suspiciously, "what he's doing that he shouldn't be."

This kind of snobbishness is poison for a church. It makes the environment feel alarmingly like the secular workplace, where people are notoriously cliquish and gossipy and judgmental. I've heard quite a few say that they went to church to find a respite from the toxicity they encounter during the week, only to discover that church felt very much the same.

Snobbishness also draws lines that separate people:

- "I'm the wise parent who did everything right; you're the clueless parent with out-of-control kids."
- "I'm the serious student of the Bible who's truly seeking God; you're just a lazy, Sunday morning church attender."
- "I'm the deeply committed Christian who's truly pursuing holiness; you're just a pop-culture addict who's filling your head with all kinds of garbage."
- "I'm the one God is blessing; you're the one who needs to get your act together."

I'm straight-up convinced that a large percentage of people drop out of church because they find it to be a big disappointment. They think it's going to be different—a place where all the lines have been erased and everyone is accepted, only to discover that the lines are there after all and made with a bold-tip marker. All of this explains the following pointed comments in Scripture:

- "My dear brothers and sisters, how can you claim to have faith in our glorious Lord Jesus Christ if you favor some people over others?" (James 2:1)
- "Yes indeed, it is good when you obey the royal law as found in the Scriptures: 'Love your neighbor as yourself.' But if you favor some people over others, you are committing a sin. You are guilty of breaking the law." (James 2:8–9)
- "Live in harmony with each other. Don't be too proud to enjoy the company of ordinary people. And don't think you know it all!" (Rom. 12:16)
- "Always be humble and gentle. Be patient with each other, making allowance for each other's faults because of your love." (Eph. 4:2)

- "Don't try to impress others. Be humble, thinking of others as better than yourselves." (Phil. 2:3)

If you're a pastor, when was the last time you preached from one of these verses? (I'm serious. You should look it up. You might be shocked at how long it's been.) Do you tell yourself that snobbishness is not really a problem in your church, that there are other topics more relevant? And then, on the (hopefully) rare occasion when a prospective family does accuse your church of being snobbish or unfriendly, do you tell yourself it's *their* problem, that they didn't take the time to really get to know your church? I am certainly not blaming pastors for the snobbishness in our churches; but having been a pastor for almost half a century, I know very well how easy it is to become "nose blind" and not notice a foul odor in your own house because you've lived with it for so long.

Sometimes spiritual nose blindness happens because of what I call the "Crazy Uncle Syndrome." Does your family have a crazy uncle (or aunt or cousin or grandparent)? You know who I'm talking about—that person you love and put up with only because he's family. You tolerate his annoying traits and overlook his offensive behavior. Sometimes in church, we do the same thing. As leaders, we peg the annoying (snobby?) people in our congregations and just accept them. Although we don't like some of what they say or do, we see them as family and just put up with it. When one of them does or says something bad, we roll our eyes and say "There he goes again" and then move on. But to a new person or family just coming in, that person is *not* family. They are *not* used to that person and are appalled by the same behavior that rolls off your back because you *are* used to it.

When I was young in ministry, I encountered a gossipy woman who kept the church in constant turmoil. She was always spreading rumors and speculations, quite a few of which were about me, the new pastor. After a few of her choice tidbits worked their way back to me, I approached one of the elders about it. He said, "Oh, that's just Florence being Florence. Everybody knows how she is and pays no attention to her." At that moment, I got a good lesson in how longtime church insiders and church newcomers can feel drastically different about bad behavior. The longtime member is virtually blind to it, while the newcomer sees it as a huge problem.

I believe it's wise to assume there *is* snobbishness in your church, even if you don't see many examples of it. With 100 percent of your people being imperfect humans, how could it *not* be there? So dig into the verses I listed above and preach against it, hard and often. Two good things will happen if you do. First, you'll be putting up a mirror to the snobby people to look into. They may or may not change, but at least you'll have done your part to help them see their sin. Second, any new people will know without question where you stand on the issue of snobbishness. That could be the thing that makes all the difference if they have a bad experience. At least they'll know you don't condone such behavior and are calling the congregation to be better than that.

One final point: If there are specific instances where snobbishness surfaces in your church, then you have to call it out. I'm not talking about policing every little haughty comment; I'm talking about the big stuff.

I'll never forget the day a Haitian man walked up to me before church one day. I'd never seen him before, so I shook his hand and welcomed him to our service. He smiled and said, "Well, this is different." I asked, "What do you mean?" He told me that he had visited another church in our community the previous Sunday and someone said to him, "We don't have any Black people in our church. You might be more comfortable someplace else." *That's* the kind of snobbishness that has to be called out and confronted. It stands against everything the Bible teaches. I'm sure it turns God's stomach. Shame on us if it doesn't turn ours.

#3

THE HYPOCRITE

Let's face it: We all have hypocritical moments. There have been times, for example, when I have preached hard against unfair criticism, only to find myself unfairly criticizing someone a few hours later. There have been times when I have been indignant at the sin of someone who ought to know better, only to realize later that I am the King of Ought to Know Better every time I sin.

There's a difference, however, between having a hypocritical moment and being a hypocrite. It's like a baseball pitcher who wins twenty games and loses five in a season. No one in their right mind would say he's a lousy pitcher, even though there were five games when he actually was pretty lousy. Pitching a bad game now and then makes you human, just like having a hypocritical moment now and then makes you human. A true hypocrite is someone who knowingly and routinely leverages fake spirituality to try to gain something.

A perfect example is found in the Christmas story. King Herod was deeply disturbed when the wise men showed up and started asking where they could find the newborn king of the Jews. "King of the Jews?" he thought. "*I'm* the king of the Jews!" He listened with growing angst as they described a star they had seen in the sky that they believed was a sign of the new king's birth. Herod, who had a paranoid streak in him a mile wide, quickly consulted the leading Jewish priests and teachers to get their take. But they only added to his fear that a new king might topple him from his throne by telling him that, yes, the Messiah was coming and, as a matter of fact, was prophesied to be born not in some far-flung outpost but right down the road in Bethlehem. In a panic, Herod gave the world as pure and horrific an example of hypocrisy as there has ever been. He called the wise men together and said, "Go to Bethlehem and search carefully for the child. And when you find him, come back, and tell me so that I can go worship him, too!" (Matt. 2:8). Of course, what he had in mind was murder, not worship.

Another example of full-bore hypocrisy can be found in Judas Iscariot. Even after he had struck a deal with the Pharisees to deliver Jesus into their hands, he sat with Jesus and the other disciples, partaking in the Last Supper and singing hymns (Matt. 26:25–30).

If you want to know why hypocrisy ranks #3 on my list of troublemakers, consider that two of the biggest villains in the whole Bible—King Herod and Judas—are its poster boys. Their hypocrisy bookended Jesus' life: Herod at the beginning and Judas at the end, resulting in two of the most heartbreaking scenes in all of history: the murder of innocent babies and the crucifixion of Jesus himself.

Thankfully, I didn't run into many hardcore hypocrites during my ministry years. I know people like to say that the church is full of hypocrites, but it really isn't. It *is* full of people who are weak and make some poor choices and, yes, have their fair share of hypocritical moments. But there aren't too many people intentionally leveraging fake spirituality to try to gain something.

One hypocrite I do remember very well was an aspiring congressman. He was a local businessman who decided to run for a seat in the House of Representatives. The Sunday after he announced his candidacy, he showed up in church, all decked out in his Sunday best, and sat toward the front—I assume so that everyone could see him. The vast majority of first-time church attenders sit in the back and try to maintain a low profile, but this man parked himself in the most conspicuous spot in the room. Make no mistake that people noticed. Everyone was shocked, because never in the man's life had he shown even a speck of interest in church.

The end of the story is that he never missed a Sunday. He was in church every single week—until the campaign came to an end and he lost the election. After that, he never set foot in our church building again (or in any other one I know of). And don't think people didn't notice that, too! There were plenty of comments about him only coming to church to try to pick up a few votes.

I remember many years ago when the owner of a lumberyard in our town made an appointment to see me. I knew him by reputation only. He was not a church attender and known to be quite rough around the edges. I couldn't imagine why he was coming to see me. It turned out that he handed me a check for $500 and said, "I'd like to make this donation to your church in return for any building or remodeling projects you might need done in the future." I handed the check back to him and said, "No thanks. Our business can't be bought. When the time comes, if we need the services you offer, we'll let you bid on the project with everyone else and go from there."

I mention this because, as distasteful as that under-the-table payment was, at least it wasn't hypocritical. The owner of that lumberyard was not leveraging fake spirituality. He was not pretending to be anything other than what he was: a businessman trying to get a leg up on his competition. In a kind of bizarre way, I appreciated that.

Which brings up an important point, and the reason why hypocrites are so dangerous. If a person is good at leveraging fake spirituality, you can be fooled—badly. Such people can worm their way into the core of the church, even into leadership positions, before you realize you're dealing with a truly bad person. Hypocrisy is like anything else. Some people are good at faking spirituality and some are not. It's that hypocrite who's really good at being a hypocrite who is deadly.

Here are some principles for protecting your church from hypocrites.

First, *be skeptical of anyone who seems too good to be true.* Everyone—and I mean *everyone*—tries to put their best foot forward when they attend a church for the first time. Someone who's caught up in a failing marriage or has an addiction or is sleeping with the boss is going to hide that fact, probably for quite a while, until trust can be developed. This is not hypocrisy; it's normal. What you need to watch out for is those who walk into your church like an actor strolls down the red carpet at the Academy Awards—those who want you to know as you shake hands for the first time how much they love Jesus and how committed they are and what sacrifices they've made in the past and how they're just here to be a blessing to your church. I've met lots of people like this, and I can tell you that they all, without exception, turned out to be a huge disappointment and sometimes a huge problem.

When I was a pastor and I met a self-proclaimed spiritual Superman, I always wondered what he was doing at our church. I mean, if he's so incredible, shouldn't he already have a church, and shouldn't he be a pillar in it? Shouldn't he be in a leadership position? Shouldn't he be out front, leading the way to greater heights than the church has ever seen? So why is he looking for a new church? Did something go wrong in his last place? Did he wear out his welcome? Did people finally figure out he was a fake, forcing him to go somewhere else and start the masquerade all over again?

If anyone shows up at your church trying hard to seem like a spiritual Superman or Wonder Woman, be very skeptical.

Second, *make humility a hallmark of your philosophy of ministry*. I remember the time a nice young couple in our church came to me with an idea. They wanted to do an annual awards banquet. Awards like "Volunteer of the Year," "Family of the Year," and, yes, even "Christian of the Year" would be given. They meant well. "This would be a great way to motivate people in our church," they said. "It would be like a high school student who knows he has a chance to be valedictorian. You just know that's going to motivate him to study even harder."

I vetoed the idea and explained that we wanted to teach people to live righteously and serve God because they love him, not because they think they might get an award at a banquet. We want people to be willing to serve humbly behind the scenes, not publicly because they want the award committee to see them and register them as a contender for some plaque or trophy. Jesus said, "Watch out! Don't do your good deeds publicly, to be admired by others, for you will lose the reward from your Father in heaven" (Matt. 6:1). He warned about showy spirituality again and again, because he knew human nature. He knew that people love a spotlight and will fall all over themselves trying to get into its beam. Just don't turn on that spotlight.

This is also the reason why we never called attention to people's special donations to the church. If someone donated $10,000 from an inheritance or $20,000 to remodel the children's wing, we thanked the giver but never revealed the person's identity to the congregation. When good deeds are done publicly and the people who do them are praised, you create the fertile soil in which hypocrisy can grow. Before long, they will be doing their good works because of the attention and praise they know they'll receive.

Third, *model humility*. You've heard it said that teams take on the personality of their coaches. I've also noticed that churches can take on the personality of their pastors. There is a church near where I live that has a pastor who is extremely bold and aggressive. He's a shouter in the pulpit and given to extreme views and statements I personally find cringe-worthy. One day, two people from his church knocked on my door. They were out evangelizing. I greeted them in a friendly manner and told them I was a Christian and attended a church I loved (though I did not tell them I was a pastor). They didn't accept that I was a Christian and started grilling me to make sure. They wanted to hear how I was saved and what I believed to confirm that I was telling the truth. This was offensive to me, so I said, still in a friendly way, "Trust me, I know if I'm a Christian or not. You have a nice day." I started to shut the door when one of them stepped forward and said "We'd like for you to give our church a try" as she shoved a pamphlet at me. At this point, I was ticked off, so I said, "Maybe you didn't hear me. I have a church I love. Goodbye." And I shut the door in their faces.

It struck me that those people were just like their pastor: loud, aggressive, and in-your-face. I definitely think there's something to the idea that groups (teams, businesses, churches) take on the personality of their leaders. So, make sure humility is being modeled in your leadership. If you're a pastor, don't always be talking about how hard you're working and what great sacrifices you're making. Don't make yourself the hero of every sermon illustration. Don't ever ask people to do messy jobs you aren't willing to do yourself. Roll up your sleeves and get your hands dirty. Be like Jesus and wash some feet. Although modeling humility won't keep hypocrites from walking into your church someday, it will create an environment where their hypocrisy stands out and marks itself as something that doesn't fit.

Not long ago, my younger brother sent me a picture. It was of him and my mom when he was about seven years old. They were sitting on a log in the Black Hills of South Dakota, holding a dead snake that was about three feet long. My brother was holding the head, and my mom was holding the tail. I emailed him back and said, "Wow! What a picture! I don't remember that happening. I would never have believed Mom would ever willingly touch a snake." He then informed me that it was a rubber snake he had bought in a Black Hills gift shop.

Sometimes things look real but aren't. It's true of snakes and super-spiritual church-goers. Your welfare could depend on you being able to tell the difference.

#2

THE MUTINEER

On April 28, 1789, angry crewmen seized control of the Royal Navy ship HMS *Bounty*. They captured Captain William Bligh and eighteen of his loyal supporters, put them into the ship's launch, and set them adrift. Amazingly, Captain Bligh navigated the launch over 3,500 nautical miles to safety and began the task of bringing the mutineers to justice, long after many of them had settled on the islands of Tahiti and Pitcairn.

It should be pointed out that the reason for the mutiny is somewhat in doubt. Captain Bligh was a difficult taskmaster. Yet, most sea captains were, and many historians argue that he was no worse than any other. The key to the crewmembers' unhappiness seems to be that they had enjoyed a five-month layover on the island of Tahiti, enjoying a hedonistic lifestyle with booze and the local women, and had lost their heart for the mission. When they got back on the ship, they were lazy and disinterested, which set them and their captain on a collision course. This would also explain why several of the mutineers returned to Tahiti after commandeering the ship.

Mutiny is one of those situations where both sides claim innocence. The mutineers scream that they were being mistreated and had no choice, and the overthrown leader screams that he was disrespected and disobeyed. There can be truth on both sides.

Mutinies are common and can happen anywhere: on ships, in boardrooms, in locker rooms, and yes, even in churches. I consider myself extremely blessed to have seen it happen only once in my forty-six years as a pastor.

We had a staff member who had been caught in some unethical behavior. He violated our well-established procedures and then covered it up by misrepresenting his actions. Simply put, he messed up and then lied about it. Believing in grace, we didn't fire him, but we gave him a stern talking-to and put him on probation for three months—which basically meant he had some hoops to jump through in order to show his commitment to restoring trust. Sadly, he did well for a few weeks and then messed up again. Yet another integrity complaint was lodged against him, which he did not deny, so we fired him.

When he was let go, our leadership made a statement that was compassionately vague. We had no desire to make him look bad (which we could easily have done), so we didn't spell out everything that had happened. He seized on this ambiguity and played the martyr. Suddenly, we were getting phone calls from people demanding to know why he was being treated so "shabbily." I personally took a call where an individual flat out told me he was going to spread the word that the leaders of our church were bullies. The mutiny was underway.

In the end, eighteen members of our church left, which is not as bad as I thought it might be when the action started. All of those who left were close friends of the person who got fired, as you would expect. But they were friends of mine too and the other elders. We had all been on good terms previously, until suddenly we weren't. This taught me a valuable lesson: In church conflicts, circumstances are often driven by emotion rather than critical thinking. A critical thinker would have said, "Hmmm, if this guy got fired, maybe he did something wrong." Instead, people react emotionally. They heard their friend's sob story (which I know was extremely slanted) and swallowed it hook, line, and sinker.

There seems to be something in people—especially Christian people—that makes them respond hotly to an injustice, and this impulse can be a good thing. But not every sob story is on the level.

Not every wounded person is a victim. Sometimes, as in the case of the man in this story, the wounds are self-inflicted. He had messed up again and again. But people who are worked up emotionally often don't process things completely. They get stuck on the notion of an injustice being perpetrated and don't think any further. From there, it's a small step to rallying their friends against the leaders they assume are the cause of the problem.

Of course, it should be said that sometimes leaders *are* at fault and *should* be challenged. In no way am I suggesting that leaders never make mistakes. But this raises an interesting question: When church members feel that their leaders are compromised in some way, that they have done something unacceptable, what should they do? Rally the troops and lead a mutiny? Leave quietly? Or perhaps something in between?

My view is that leading a mutiny against the leaders is almost never the right choice. I say "almost never" because maybe someone can think of a scenario where I would change my mind. I'll at least concede that very slim possibility. But I've been around a long time, and I've never seen a situation where I thought creating all-out war in the church was the right choice. The apostle Paul said that everything in the church should be done decently and in order (1 Cor. 14:40). The damage done to people's faith, their relationships, and the church's reputation in the community would be far more harmful than any positive result that could come from a mutiny. This is partly because, once a church war gets started, it quickly veers away from the original issues and becomes nasty and petty. I've never seen a situation where this wasn't the case. In fact, many church fights deteriorate to the point that those involved completely forget what the original disagreement was about! Therefore, I believe the right choice for church members who are frustrated with their leaders is to communicate their feelings respectfully; and if they can't live with the outcome, then leave. Find somewhere else to worship.

Many years ago, I met a man who came to our church because he had a problem with the leaders of his former church. Believe me, anytime that happened, I wanted to know the scoop. I wanted to know what I was getting into with that person. Was it a legitimate disagreement that caused him to leave his former church, or something else? Was he a principled Christian or a petty malcontent who was now bringing his gripes into *our* fellowship? It turned out the man felt the elders had compromised the Scriptures with a couple of their decisions. Fine. My question to him was still: "Why did you leave? Why didn't you stay and stand up for what you believe is a biblical truth?" He gave a mature answer. He said, "Out of respect for the body of Christ, I chose not to raise a ruckus. I decided to leave quietly and worship elsewhere and let God decide what should happen in that place. If he wants to bring about change there, he can certainly do it."

Although that case was a false alarm, it's often not. So, what do you do if you're leading a church and a mutineer rises up and starts rallying the members against you?

First, *find a mirror and take a good, long, hard look into it*. This is critical. When church problems arise, far too many people (including leaders) fail to consider the possibility they actually might be at fault. They're so busy digging in and pleading their case to anyone who will listen, they fail to consider that maybe *they* are in the wrong, at least somewhat if not entirely. I recommend that you pray along with David, "Lord, point out anything in me that offends you" (Ps. 139:24), and then respond humbly and obediently if he does.

Second, *if you believe you're in the right, then formulate a clear, concise statement that explains why*. One of the worst things that can happen when a church fight erupts is to have members of the leadership team all saying something different. Understand, I am not suggesting that anyone be muzzled or that the leaders shouldn't be honest. Whatever statement the leaders come up with should be truthful and fully address the issues at hand. It should not be cryptic or spiteful or threatening. Nor should it violate anyone's privacy. The leaders will inevitably know things most members of the congregation don't know, but that does not mean they should *tell* everything they know. The object here is to be open and unambiguous about the leaders' position on the matters at hand.

Third, *be willing to bend without breaking*. Scripture must never be compromised. But if the issues causing the problem relate more to the church's methodology or structure or culture, then there could well be some room for flexibility. If, for example, you've started a new program that has a large number of people up in arms, it might be wise to rethink that program, modify it, or perhaps chuck it altogether. Don't be hard-headed. Don't stuff cotton in your ears. If people are unhappy with what's happening, and it's not a biblical issue, be willing to reconsider. There were many times during my ministry years when I was forced to face the cold, hard truth about one of my ideas—that it wasn't nearly as good as I first thought.

Fourth, *refuse to be intimidated*. If you conclude that the issue at the heart of the trouble is a hill worth dying on, then stand firm. Just remember that things will likely get messy. People might leave. Never forget that this could be God's way of performing surgery on the congregation. No one wants surgery. It's painful and often involves serious recovery time. But we all know that the patient is much healthier afterward. The worst thing church leaders can do is compromise their heartfelt beliefs in an effort to keep people from leaving. What you end up with is people in your church who have now discovered that they can control you by threatening to declare a mutiny. From that point on, *they* will be running the church.

Finally, *if the mutiny goes forward, maintain your Christian witness*. Whatever you say or do, say it or do it in love. Don't let yourself be provoked. Don't get sucked into an exchange of verbal hand grenades. Don't start giving people the cold shoulder because you think they might be against you. Yes, speak to the situation and defend your convictions as needed, but don't get catty and badmouth the mutineer or their followers behind their backs. Keep in mind that it doesn't matter how right you are on the issue at the center of the controversy; you discredit yourself and become a detriment to the kingdom when you do anything that dishonors Christ. I've seen too many situations where church leaders were wrong even when they were right.

To close this chapter, I want to return to that mutiny on the *Bounty*. When those mutineers set Captain Bligh and his loyal crew members adrift on the sea, they thought they had won. But the story was actually far from over. When Captain Bligh reached England in 1790, he reported what had happened. Promptly, HMS *Pandora* was dispatched to bring the mutineers to justice. Several were captured and tried, and those who were found to be guilty were hanged.

This is a good reminder that it's best not to draw conclusions about a situation until the end of the story has been written. A church mutiny can seem like the ultimate disaster when it's in progress, but God has proven that he can bring good out of bad. When all was said and done, many a church leader has looked back on a mutiny and realized that God used it all for good.

#1

THE LIAR

Being #1 is usually thought of as a good thing.

It's great to be #1 in your class, in your league, on the bestseller list, on the music charts, or in the heart of that person who's #1 in *your* heart.

There are, however, a few lists you don't want to sit atop.

You don't want to be #1 on the FBI's most wanted list, Mr. Blackwell's Worst-Dressed list, or Rotten Tomatoes' worst actor (or actress) list.[18] You especially don't want to be #1 on this list of biggest troublemakers.

Every church staff has a list of biggest troublemakers in the congregation they serve. Maybe they've never actually written it down. Maybe they never talk about it when non staff members are within earshot. But I guarantee that in every church there is a church member who gets talked about more than any other around the church office, because he (or she) causes more headaches than any other, drains more energy than any other, offends more people than any other, or incites more anger than any other, and ultimately tarnishes the church's witness more than any other. I served five churches as a full-time pastor, and in every one of them I had a number one biggest troublemaker. If you had asked me in any of those churches to pick the one person who frustrated me the most and did the most damage to the body, I could have picked him or her in two seconds flat.

Trust me, this is a distinction you don't want.

How would you stand before God someday and explain it? What would you say if he looked you in the eye and said, "Why were you such a pain? Why were you working against me at every turn? Why did you cause my bride such misery?" There are many things I wouldn't want to have to try to explain to God on Judgment Day. Why I abused his bride is right at the top of the list.

There is one thing that all of the worst troublemakers I had in the various churches I served had in common: They all played fast and loose with the truth. They had other issues too, make no mistake. But all of them—without exception—stretched, twisted, manipulated, obscured, or simply denied the truth when it served their purpose. They were liars.

This shouldn't come as a surprise. It was a lie that triggered the very first sin all the way back in the Garden of Eden (Gen. 3:1–7). From day one, Satan believed that nothing would serve his goal of disrupting the purposes of God like twisting or misrepresenting the truth. And he's never stopped doing it. You can pick just about any incident in history that involved conflict, unrest, or injustice and, if you peel away the layers down to the heart of it, you'll find something false: a myth, a fabrication, an exaggeration, a misrepresentation, a subterfuge, an evasion, an inaccuracy, a forgery, a trick, a betrayal, or a distortion.

There are three reasons why a lie is so effective at instigating trouble.

First, *people are gullible*. How else would you explain *rumpology*? A rumpologist examines the shape, folds, dimples, and creases of your posterior and then uses that information to predict your future. Astrologer and rumpologist Jacqueline Stallone (yes, Sylvester's mom) used to give a complete rumpology report for a mere $600 ($300 per cheek).[19]

If people will believe in rumpology, they'll believe anything. I doubt you could dream up a lie so crazy that somebody somewhere wouldn't believe it if you act convincing and say it often enough.

Second, *people are good actors*. I once had a young woman in her twenties sit in front of my desk and tell me she had been diagnosed with terminal cancer. She wept uncontrollably, using a dozen tissues to wipe real tears. She absolutely broke my heart as she wailed about never being able to have children or take care of her parents in their old age. It turned out that she was emotionally disturbed, that she craved attention and had a long history of fabricating scenarios to get people's sympathy. She didn't have cancer any more than I had a tomato plant growing out of the top of my head, but she had me believing. I don't think an Oscar-winning actor could have been more convincing.

Some people are lousy liars, but lots of people are really good at it. And people who are good at it generally know they're good at it and do not fail to use the talent to their advantage. And when a good liar encounters someone who is gullible, something bad is bound to happen.

Third, *a lie can be crafted to fit any situation*. Obviously, you can state the opposite of the truth. But you can also exaggerate the truth, withhold part of the truth, present the truth out of context, misquote the truth, state your opinion as if it's the truth, repeat a rumor as if it's the truth, or simply keep quiet when you know the truth. Lies are like shoes: If one style doesn't go with your outfit, you can be sure there's another one that will. Perhaps no tool of Satan is so versatile.

Finally, *the temptation to lie is so strong that sometimes even good people fall prey to it*. Abraham lied. Peter, who was part of Jesus' inner circle, lied. Ananias and Sapphira (Acts 5:1–10), who appear to have been upstanding members of the early church, lied. And make no mistake, the lies of good church people can be just as devastating as the lies of even the most ill-intentioned troublemakers, as the following story illustrates.

I had just become the pastor of a church that selected its elders by a vote of the members. The Bible doesn't stipulate how elders are to be chosen, so this congregation did it by asking the members to nominate candidates and then vote on them by private ballot, yes or no. There was a certain percentage of yes votes the candidate had to receive to be approved.

I hadn't been the pastor at that church for three months before I realized we had a bad elder. He was always grumpy and had a quick temper. He was the kind of guy everyone walks on eggshells around for fear of setting him off. He was so grumpy that when the movie *Grumpy Old Men* came out, I expected to see his face on the poster. But worse than being grumpy and ill-tempered, he had questionable ethics. Tales of his dishonesty in business were many. I had several old-timers warn me never to trust him. I also began to realize that he was going to oppose me on any new ideas I might have to move the church forward. He found something wrong with everything I suggested, and that's not an exaggeration. I don't recall him ever supporting even one of my ideas.

One day, he was accused of making a brutally unkind, sexually oriented comment about a prominent young woman in our church. He denied it of course. But there were several trustworthy witnesses. I had no doubt whatsoever that he was guilty. You'll often hear preachers talking about brush fires breaking out in the church that have to be put out. This wasn't a brush fire; it was a full-scale forest fire. Word got around quickly, and people were outraged that an elder would say such a thing.

One evening, shortly after this accusation exploded, I was discussing the situation with another elder who had become a close friend. I said, "What I can't figure out is how Joe ever became an elder in the first place. Everybody knows what a difficult person he is and almost nobody trusts him. It just doesn't make sense that such good, level-headed people would vote for him to be an elder." My friend didn't comment.

That night around eleven o'clock, my doorbell rang. It was that same elder I'd talked to earlier in the evening who'd had nothing to say in response to my expression of disbelief that the congregation could have made such a troublemaker an elder. We walked into my living room and sat down. I noticed that he had tears in his eyes.

This is what he said.

"Mark, I have to get something off my chest, or I'm going to go crazy. The reason Joe is an elder is because I told a lie. On the Sunday he was voted on ten years ago, I was asked to tally the ballots. When he fell well short of the number he needed to be approved, I felt sorry for him. I thought he would be embarrassed to know so many people didn't want him. I thought it might break his spirit and make him want to leave the church, since we haven't had a nominee fail to be approved by the congregation in many, many years. So when I was asked for the tally, I lied and said he was approved by a comfortable margin. I thought it would encourage him, that being an elder would cause him to up his game and be a better person. I was pretty sure no one would doublecheck my count, and I was right. But it didn't work out the way I hoped. For all these years, he's been a horrible leader who's hurt the church and made all of our lives miserable, and every time something like this happens, I just feel sick to my stomach because I know it's all my fault."

In my view, lying is the greatest threat to the body of Christ. Lies hurt people deeply. They spark anger and destroy relationships. They cause divisions. They crush morale and poison the atmosphere. They confuse and misdirect people who are searching for truth. They stain the reputation of the bride of Christ and provide ammunition to the enemies of the faith. And mark this down: Lies that are told with compassionate motives, as was the case in the story I just shared, are no better than lies that are told with evil motives. Satan couldn't care less if you're trying to help things by lying; he will never miss an opportunity to use a lie to undermine the cause of Christ.

When it is discovered that someone has intentionally obscured or twisted the truth, wise leaders will act quickly, especially if that person is in a position of authority or leadership. Twice in my years as a pastor we had to fire someone on our staff for lying. Once we had to remove a church member for telling a particularly egregious lie and then threatening to harm the staff member who exposed her. Numerous times we had to sit regular church members down and talk to them about some lie they told. None of these actions and conversations were easy. In some cases, they were gut-wrenching. But we felt that lying was the single most dangerous sin we faced. When people are allowed to lie and get away with it, there will be bondage, suspicion, mistrust, fear, and animosity. What chance does the church have of being what God has called it to be if it is allowed to become a place of such darkness? But when we make truth a priority, we are set free from these things. Mark Roberts said it well: "The path of truthfulness is the narrow path in today's world, by far the road less traveled. But it is the way of God, the way of significance, the way of freedom."[20] Jesus said it best: "You shall know the truth and the truth will set you free" (John 8:32).

When pastors are interviewed for a potential ministry, they ask all kinds of questions about the church's history, demographics, worship style, pay and benefits package, and so on. And rightfully so; such things are important. A few years ago, I came to the conclusion that the most important question a pastor can ask is the one I never asked in all my interviews for various ministries: "Is this church a community where the truth is valued, fought for, and defended in matters large and small?" How can there be a more important question than this?

Jesus said, "I am the Way, the Truth, and the Life" (John 14:6). When we value the truth, we value Jesus. Consider the ramifications of this. We can say we love Jesus all day long, but if we don't value the truth on a day-to-day basis in matters large and small, then our claim is a hoax. A church might have the greatest building, the coolest technology, and the hippest band in the land, but if the truth is optional, if people are allowed to play fast and loose with the truth without being called on it, then we are more allies of Satan than servants of Christ.

Whatever you may believe in and fight for as a church leader, if the truth is not at the top of the list, you need to step back and rethink your priorities.

PART 4

THE DEFENSE

Some of us prefer mercy to justice, grace to law, the staff to the rod. Others prefer the opposite. But, as shepherds, we need to occupy both roles comfortably. The parents who tuck their children into bed with a story, a prayer, and a gentle kiss are the same parents who check the alarm system, lock the doors, and respond swiftly if the dog barks.[21]

Timothy S. Laniak, *While Shepherds Watch Their Flocks*

1

CHOOSE YOUR LEADERS CAREFULLY

Earlier in this book, I stated that it's impossible to keep your church troublemaker-free. Unfortunately, a certain percentage of the people in your community fit the profiles I wrote about in the first three sections. There are lots of lotharios, hypocrites, control freaks, and liars out there. So, when you promote your church to your community and invite people to come, you're inviting them just as surely as you're inviting those humble, godly souls who might fit the profile of the perfect church member.

I've always thought that the way to become a billionaire would be to invent a "troublemaker detector" that would look something like the metal detector you step through when you go through security at the airport. You could put one at every entrance to your church building—and when the red light flashed, security would step in and frog-march the offender out the door before they could do any harm.

But that's a pipe dream. The best you can do is to put a plan in place to minimize both the number and the influence of troublemakers in your church. Step number one in that effort is to choose your church leaders carefully.

The statement I'm about to make might sound strange, but it's absolutely true: When you see a church encumbered and beleaguered by ongoing troubles, it's not the people causing the trouble who are to blame. It's the leaders—or as I'll refer to them from here forward, the elders. Either they've turned a blind eye or they've bungled their response. You can't expect troublemakers not to cause trouble; it's what they do. But you have every right to expect that the people you put in place as elders will protect and guard the flock. Paul said to the elders in Ephesus, "So guard yourselves and God's people. Feed and shepherd God's flock—his church, purchased with his own blood—over which the Holy Spirit has appointed you as elders" (Acts 20:28). I'd say it's true 100 percent of the time that when your church body is continually in upheaval because people are misbehaving, you don't have a troublemaker problem—you have a leadership problem.

Here are two serious mistakes I have seen that lead to weak leadership in a church.

Mistake #1: Making It Too Easy to Become an Elder

In 1 Timothy 3:1–7 and Titus 1:6–9, Paul lays out specific qualifications for elders. Depending on how you count and separate some of the phrases, there are at least twenty-one requirements. Some are basic, the kinds of expectations you'd place on almost anyone, such as not being violent or wild and rebellious. But other requirements raise the bar considerably higher, such as being above reproach or able to teach. I believe the reason God was so detailed in his qualifications for elders is because he knew the health of his church and the safety of his people would rise or fall on their actions.

The problem is that in many churches the qualifications Paul lays out are largely ignored. They're given little more than a wink and a nod when the time comes to choose new leaders. People are chosen simply because they're well liked or because they're big givers or they've been successful in business.

As I write this, I'm thinking of a man who might be among the top three worst elders I've ever known. He was already an elder when I was interviewed and hired by the church, so I assumed he was well qualified. But as the first few months rolled by, I began to realize he wasn't qualified at all; in fact, he was a real problem—

someone who triggered conflict and resentment because of his overbearing personality and sharp tongue. One day, I happened to be talking privately with a church member I had come to respect and trust, and I asked, "How did that guy ever become an elder?" My conversation partner hung his head and said, "I'm ashamed to say it, but a lot of us saw what a successful businessman he is, and we thought it would be great to have someone with that kind of business sense on our team."

I was stunned. Nowhere in Paul's list of qualifications does it say, "Must be successful in business." Rather, Paul's qualifications are all about integrity, spirituality, and temperament. I'm not saying it isn't great to have savvy businesspeople on your team, but not if they flunk the biblical tests.

Some might say, "But we don't have enough people who are truly qualified. We have to lower our standards a little to make a team."

No, you don't. There is no scenario in which it's okay to appoint unqualified elders. If you don't have people who are qualified for the eldership, then you need to get serious about leadership development. Identify people with potential and start teaching and training them. You may have to run the church with a business committee temporarily while you work on this. But whatever you do, don't lower the standards God has set. You will eventually regret it if you do.

Here are three reasons why it's important to be strict when applying Paul's qualifications to potential leaders.

First, *the unity and morale of your leadership team is at stake.* It's true of all teams, from churches to businesses to sports: if you get someone in the mix who doesn't fit, who doesn't have the right attitude, isn't on board with the vision, or simply isn't a team player, then it's going reduce the effectiveness of your team. At moments when it's critical that everyone pulls together, you could instead have division and bickering. I know too well the feeling of walking out of a meeting with my blood boiling because someone, who should never have been on the team in the first place, had seemed to be intentionally obtuse and uncooperative. That's not to say you couldn't also have disagreements if everyone on the team *is* fully qualified; but because everyone on the team is fully qualified according to the Scriptures, the tone and level of maturity will be greater, thus making the likelihood of finding harmonious consensus that much greater.

Second, *bad leadership can't be hidden and will become the identity of your church.* I'm sure you can think of restaurants or businesses you prefer not to visit because the service is bad, the employees are rude, or the place is dirty. Any business can be caught in a bad moment, but when you find that slipshoddiness is a pattern, then you're not looking at bad employees—you're looking at bad management or leadership. No organization is ever going to rise above the level of its leadership. And make no mistake, churches get bad reputations just like businesses do. In the city where I live, there are several churches known to be "troubled" or "dysfunctional." I've never attended them, but I've heard about them. Everybody has.

Third, *it's important to strictly apply Paul's qualifications for elders, because doing so plugs the holes and fills the cracks that might otherwise be an opening for Satan.* An example would be a man who loves the Lord and has many great qualities but struggles with an explosive temper. Paul says that an elder should be self-controlled (1 Tim. 3:2), but let's say the guy's good qualities are numerous, so those making the decision to add or not add him to the team decide not to hold his hot temper against him. They figure he will work on it as time goes by, so they approve him to be an elder. Of course, Satan will see that one overlooked weakness and zero in on it. You can take it to the bank that this leader's temperament will be sorely tested.

Of course, I'm not suggesting that someone has to be perfect before being allowed to be an elder. But God in his wisdom has identified the key qualities the leaders of his church are going to need and laid them out for us in no uncertain terms. To be soft on those qualifications is to open the door for unqualified people to be at the helm of your church in some future moment of crisis when qualified leaders may be all that separates you from complete disaster.

Mistake #2: Making It Too Hard to Remove a Leader

Even if you manage to approve only highly qualified people for your eldership team, you can still have a problem because people change. During my years as a pastor, I saw two elders move from qualified to unqualified while serving. Let me tell you about one of those cases.

The man I'm referring to was in business and ran into hard times. The economy was bad, and he may well have made some unwise financial decisions. The result was that his company, which was his lifelong dream, was tanking and taking a toll on his emotional state and his marriage. This man, who had always been so positive and upbeat, was suddenly sullen. In meetings, he was all gloom and doom, finding something wrong with every idea. Even his family members spoke of how difficult it was to be around him. Clearly, he was no longer qualified to lead the church. Among other things, he had become quarrelsome (1 Tim. 3:3) and was no longer leading his family well (1 Tim. 3:4).

What do you do in a situation like this?

In the case of this man, the problem solved itself when his business went belly-up, and he and his wife moved. But if he hadn't moved, we would have had to deal with the situation somehow. Here are two suggestions for setting up your church leadership to deal with this kind of problem.

First, *avoid giving people lifetime appointments to the eldership.* This used to be more common than it is now, but there are still churches that do this. I served a church that had a "once an elder, always an elder" approach to leadership and it was problematic. People change, as I've already pointed out. But people also grow old and became less physically or mentally able to handle the often demanding and stressful job of leading a church. I remember one case where I needed to tell an elder about a problem that had arisen, but because he was elderly and in bad health, I just didn't have the heart to do it. I felt bad, trapped between duty and compassion. But this is what happens when you give people lifetime appointments. You invite awkward situations with no easy answers.

I recommend approving a first-time elder for one year only. At the end of that year, do an evaluation and if there are no problems, then move forward with a two- or three-year term of service.

Second, *build an evaluation procedure that has teeth into your system*. There are certain basic questions that should be asked as elders approach the end of their current term:

- Do they consistently attend meetings?
- Do they faithfully attend church services and activities?
- Do they give generously and consistently?
- Do they demonstrate humility by serving?
- Are their marriages healthy? Do they maintain a positive working relationship with the pastor and staff?
- Do they live by faith and demonstrate a positive outlook?
- Are they supportive of the church's vision?
- Are they growing spiritually?

All those invited to be elders should have to agree to allow their fellow elders to scrutinize them along these lines before they're allowed to begin a new term. Although evaluations like this hardly ever happen, the idea is not unreasonable. Read the questions again.

They are simple and basic—the minimum of what you would expect of an elder. Yet they create an opportunity to address growing problems that otherwise would probably slide on by. Anyone who shows a reluctance to be evaluated shouldn't be put in such an important leadership role.

Near where I live there used to be a restaurant I loved. When I first started going there, it was a first-class operation. But as time went by, I noticed the quality slipping. One day, I was handed a different menu that did not include my favorite entrée. I asked the server (whom I knew well) what was up, and she rolled her eyes and whispered that the owners were having financial problems and were cutting costs. "How can they be having financial problems?" I asked. "This place is packed every day." She just shook her head and shrugged.

Over the next few months, the quality of the food and the service continued to deteriorate and customers grew more and more scarce. One day, as I was driving by, I saw a *FOR SALE* sign in front of the building and felt sad. I don't know what happened behind the scenes of that business, but I know this: the building was nice, the recipes were great, the servers were on the ball, and the customers loved the place. That leaves the people at the top as the prime suspects.

In *The 21 Indispensable Qualities of a Leader*, John Maxwell wrote, "Everything rises and falls on leadership."[22] Outside of the Bible, those might be the six most important words ever spoken about leadership. When you see a business or a church that's thriving and growing, it's never an accident. It's usually because somebody at the top is leading and managing well. And when you see one that's troubled and dysfunctional, it's usually because someone at the top isn't.

Choose your leaders carefully.

2

SHAPE YOUR CULTURE INTENTIONALLY

When a sports team, college or pro, gets into a prolonged rut and loses most of its games, the coach is probably going to get fired. When that happens, the fans, commentators, and most importantly, the new coach will talk about how the culture needs to be changed. What, specifically, does the coach mean by that? Simply put, the culture is the standard of what's acceptable and what isn't.

When Eliah Drinkwitz became the new head football coach at the University of Missouri, he took over a program in the doldrums. In just his third game, his team upset the highly ranked, defending National Champion LSU Tigers, which prompted a round of interviews on national sports talk shows. One interviewer asked him if he hoped this surprising victory would open the door to more victories in the near future. Coach Drinkwitz responded by informing the host that *hope* was a word no one in his program was allowed to use: "We don't hope around here. We expect."

As a Mizzou fan, I loved it. I know every successful leader understands that if you keep doing what you've always done, you'll keep getting what you've always gotten. New standards, new attitudes, and new behaviors, and yes, sometimes even new words have to be introduced and embraced in order to create a more positive culture.

The same is true in the church.

If you're in a congregation where troublemakers feel at home and continually keep things stirred up, then you simply have to change the culture. If you're a new pastor coming in, then you might think that just getting rid of the old pastor and bringing in someone as wonderful as you will be enough to turn the tide. Don't count on it. Even if people behave for a while, it's likely not because they've all repented of their troublemaking ways. More likely, it's because they're getting to know you and trying to make a good impression. (Yes, even troublemakers want to make a good impression on the new pastor.) This is commonly called the "honeymoon period." Although honeymoons are real, they don't last long—maybe a few weeks at best. Most pastors can tell you the exact moment when their honeymoon ended.

But it's not just troubled churches that can need a culture change. Sometimes happy, harmonious churches do too. For example, some churches are held back by mediocrity. They are disorganized, communication is poor, volunteers are undependable, and worst of all, no one is held accountable in these areas. The members may get along well, but there's almost no chance the church will grow (unless it's in a small town where there's no competition), because unchurched people generally don't choose poor quality over good quality. No one does. This kind of church needs a culture change just as much as one that is strife torn.

Make no mistake: culture change is powerful. I'm not sure there's anything church leaders can do that will produce greater and more lasting change.

When I was thirty-four, I moved from the Midwest, where I was born and raised and had lived my entire life, to Florida. Pastoring over a thousand miles from the part of the country I knew best caused me to lose touch with many of the people and churches I was familiar with. I'll never forget being back in the Midwest several years after I moved to Florida. I happened to be passing by a small church that had been well known back in the day for being dysfunctional and deeply troubled. I couldn't believe the beautiful new facility that graced the property and the size of the campus. I started asking questions and learned that the congregation was seen as one of the outstanding churches in the entire area. People drove from far and wide to attend there. I was thrilled to learn what had happened and knew one thing: That church had undergone a profound culture change. I don't know who led the way or how long it took, but it obviously happened. You may know of similar situations where churches that had been in the doldrums for years suddenly began to come alive. I promise you: culture change was a part of that.

Of course, the culture of any team or organization won't change on its own. It won't happen by accident or by wishing on a star or using the power of positive thinking. It won't even change if you pray about it, if prayer is all you plan to do. Culture change demands that you be intentional. Here are six steps you can take that will help you reshape the culture of your church.

Step #1: Envision the Culture You Want

When I was much younger and taking my golf game very seriously, I read Jack Nicklaus's book *Golf My Way*. One of the tips I got from that book was to visualize the shot I wanted to make during my practice swing. Simply address the ball, take a nice smooth practice swing, and picture the ball flying through the air and landing where I wanted it to. I was skeptical at first but found it really helped. I actually made better golf shots if I took a moment to imagine a good shot instead of just stepping up and whacking the ball.

I'm convinced that visualization is critical to success in life as well as golf. You stand a much better chance of ending up with a result you'll like if you spend some time picturing the result you want. Visualizing yourself as being healthy and fit will help you say no to that bedtime bowl of ice cream. Visualizing yourself someday being in a godly marriage with a faithful spouse will help you say no to the womanizer or shameless flirt who asks you out. Visualizing yourself being financially healthy in retirement will help you put that little bit extra into savings instead of blowing it.

The first step to shaping a new culture for your church is to picture it in your mind:

- Imagine a church where the elders are humble, godly, and wise.
- Imagine a church where people treat one another with respect and embrace diversity.
- Imagine a church where forgiveness is offered to those who mess up.
- Imagine a church where outsiders are welcome.
- Imagine a church where excellence is the norm rather than the exception.
- Imagine a church where Jesus is the focus instead of just a name on a website or in a brochure.
- Imagine a church where troublemakers are confronted and held accountable, according to the Scriptures.

The possibilities are endless, but you must identify them and begin to build that church in your mind. I dare say that every great accomplishment of humanity—every great invention or innovation—started out as a well-developed idea between someone's ears.

Step #2: Get Your Staff and Leadership Team on Board

Culture change happens from the top down, so if your upper-level leaders are not on board, then you can forget it. But getting them on board may not be as easy as you think. It's possible that they have either helped shape the current unhealthy culture or tolerated it and grown comfortable with it. When you start talking about changing it, they could easily dig in their heels. They might not agree with you that it even needs to be changed. They might see the task as being too big and therefore hopeless. Or—and this is very common—they might be wary of the changes *they* would have to make in order to bring about a change in the culture. They might, for example, be wary of having to be more confrontational with difficult people. Or they might be reluctant to embrace new policies and procedures that would demand more of their time. I offer two suggestions for getting your leadership team on board for a culture change.

First, *don't move too fast.* Don't cram the idea down their throats. Instead, start talking about it as opportunities arise. When negative things happen that demonstrate the need for a better culture, point them out. Explain how problems could be greatly reduced if only the culture was different. Culture change is a long process, often taking several years. When attempts to accomplish it fail, it's often because things were rushed.

Second, *open your team's mind to how things are done in other churches.* Some church leaders have lived their entire lives in one church and may not be aware that there are better ways of doing things. I'll always fondly remember the time the entire leadership team of the church I was serving visited a larger, fast-growing church, just to see how they did things and to pick the brains of their leaders. We left there with a greatly expanded vision for our church and some ideas that worked beautifully for us when we adapted them to our situation. The point is that you don't just have to tell your team about the benefits of an improved culture. You can show them.

Step #3: Weave Your Vision into Your Preaching and Teaching

One of the great privileges a pastor has is the opportunity to speak to his people often. It's hard to overestimate the importance of this when you're trying to bring about change. You get to choose the topics and frame the narrative, and you get to make your case directly to them. I do, however, have a couple of suggestions.

First, *don't be heavy-handed.* So many pastors make this mistake. They harangue their people. They harp on their pet topic to the point that people get tired of hearing about it. Be a little more savvy than that. Remember, when Jesus was teaching the multitudes, he didn't conk them on the head with his message. Instead, he used parables—compelling little stories that drew them in, sparked their imaginations, and elicited questions. There are countless stories and passages in the Bible that will give you an opportunity to weave in a bit of your vision for a better church. Although it might just be a comment or two out of a thirty-minute message, over time, if you are thoughtful, you can shape the thinking of your people.

Second, *be positive.* All the reasons why the culture of your church needs to change are negative. But you can't sound negative! You can't let yourself whine or complain when you talk about the need for change, or people will get the idea that you're down on the church. You're *not* down on the church. You *love* the church, which is why you want to make it better. Go back and read Paul's letters and see how his love for the congregation he's writing to comes through loud and clear, even as he addresses problems and calls people to step up their game.

Step #4: Introduce New Terminology

Words are important. The Bible compares the tongue to a small rudder that can change the course of a large ship, even in a mighty wind (James 3:4). You will be wise to apply this truth to culture change. By thoughtfully choosing one word over another, you can shape the way people react to your message of change. For example, instead of talking about changing something, speak instead about upgrading it. Change is something people generally don't like, but who doesn't like an upgrade? If you've ever been upgraded to a better seat on an airplane or a fancier rental car or a newer computer by your employer, then you know what a great feeling it is. By the way, if the change you're thinking about making *isn't* a clear upgrade, then you probably shouldn't be making it.

Another word I like is *friendly*. Instead of saying, "We're going to change how we do our worship service," say, "We're going to make our service more worship-friendly." Of course, if you do that, then you must be able to explain *how* the service is going to be more worship-friendly. People won't be fooled by words alone. Here are a few more words and phrases that will help you as you try to navigate change:

- *Elevate*
- *Improve*
- *Update*
- *Enhance*
- *Expand*
- *Sharpen*
- *Broaden*
- *Strengthen*
- *Make strides*
- *Perk up*

At the same time, there are some terms you should steer clear of. For example, if you talk about "fixing" something, this implies that it's broken—and it may well be! But that terminology is going to sting whoever is serving in that area. The same is true of a word like *dysfunctional*. You may certainly have some ministry in your church that's dysfunctional, but what does it say to those serving in that area if you refer to their ministry that way?

When you choose your words, consider what I call the "lean factor." Some words are compelling and cause people to lean in, while others are off-putting and cause them to lean back. You want people leaning in and showing interest, not pulling back and setting up walls of resistance.

Step #5: Start Small

The last thing you want to do is try to change everything all at once. To do that, you would have to impose a lot of unfamiliar policies and procedures that will cause your people to feel like strangers in their own church. The wise approach is to start small. Find some area of your ministry that needs attention and think about how to upgrade it. My suggestion is to start with an area where improvement is truly needed, where it's not a matter of opinion, some area that everybody knows needs attention. If you can truly upgrade that area, then those affected by it will be happy. And when people are happy with one change, they're likely to be more open to another.

Step #6: Be Patient

For the last thirty-plus years, I've lived fifteen hours by car from my childhood hometown where my mother still lives. A fifteen-hour drive sounds terrible, doesn't it? But my wife and I enjoy it. Why? Because over the years, we've found a dozen or more restaurants, shops, outlets, bookstores, and record stores along the way that we love to visit. Granted, those wonderful places turn our fifteen-hour trip into a two day trip, but that's okay. We've figured out that the journey is fun if you enjoy the stops along the way.

This is how you must approach culture change. It's a long trip, so don't be in a hurry to get there. Enjoy the stops along the way. Take time to mark the moments when you see real progress and celebrate them with your people. I believe that one of the reasons pastors stay in their churches only about four years on average is because they are too impatient. They want to see results *now*. When it doesn't happen, they convince themselves that a better opportunity where progress happens more quickly awaits them somewhere else.

One of my favorite things is to see a preacher come into a church that has had a revolving door of pastors for decades. Everybody thinks he's just making a pit stop on his way to a better opportunity, but then he surprises them. He settles in and gets to work actually leading the church, developing a vision, and sharing it with his people. One day you wake up and the church is completely different. The culture has changed. It's healthy, strong, and doing ministry on a scale never before seen—and it's growing! People actually want to be a part of it.

What about all those pastors who passed through that revolving door without seeing anything significant happen? It's so interesting to hear them explain why the situation was different when they pastored there.

No, it wasn't different.

The difference is that a pastor finally came along who understood the importance of being patient and committing to the long haul. Again, think of the churches you know of that were going nowhere and are now vibrant and growing. I dare say that, in every case, there was a patient pastor with a positive vision at the center of that transformation.

If you're a basketball fan, you may remember Dikembe Mutombo, who played eighteen seasons in the NBA. He was a fine player who was known for one thing above all else. When an opposing player attacked the basket, he would often swat the player's shot away and then wag his finger at the player as if to say, "No, no, no. Don't bring that in here!" His finger wag became such a signature move that you can actually start typing "Dikembe" into your internet search engine and "Dikembe Mutombo finger wag" will come up automatically. Watch today's generation of young players in both college and the NBA, and you'll see finger wags all over the place.

A healthy culture does for a church what Dikembe Mutombo did for his team: it prevents those who would attack the body from having their way. Troublemakers rarely make much headway in a church with a healthy culture. They may try to start a fire, but a healthy culture that has been cultivated patiently over time will provide little, if any, kindling. This is because people in a church with a healthy culture become protective of it. They love being part of a happy, healthy family, and they don't want to see it ruined. I've even seen cases where the happy members of a healthy church will police troublemakers themselves without the church leaders having to get involved. "No, no, no! Don't bring that in here!" is a clear message to a troublemaker that he needs to either move on or shape up.

With or without the finger wag.

3

PICK YOUR BATTLES THOUGHTFULLY

I struggled with the title for this chapter. I thought maybe "pick your battles" sounded a bit too militaristic for a book about church life. Then I remembered how 1 Timothy 6:12 talks about the life of faith being a fight. As I reflected on some of the perfectly horrible conflicts I had to deal with during my years as a pastor, suddenly the word *battles* didn't seem inappropriate at all. As you can see, I decided to go with it.

I've said in this book that no church is ever going to be completely trouble-free. Wherever there are people with different levels of maturity and different personalities, there will be squabbles and turmoil. I'm an advocate of dealing with such things in a timely manner and getting them resolved. The key is knowing what situations are serious enough to need some kind of intervention and which ones are not.

When I got married, an older man who was a great influence in my life told me that the difference between a happily married couple and an unhappily married couple was eyesight. When I gave him a blank stare, he smiled and explained: "If you're going to see every little imperfection in each other, you're doomed. You've got to be a little bit blind." He was right, of course, and the same is true of church life. Yes, you want to develop and maintain a healthy culture, but you need to pick your battles thoughtfully. You can't call an emergency elders' meeting every time someone in your church gets testy and says something rude. Sometimes you just have to let things go and trust that the culture you're building, as well as people's faith and belief in godly values, will enable them to work through their bumpy moments in a positive way.

Here are some questions you can ask that will help you pick your battles wisely.

Question #1: Does the Problem Involve False Doctrine?

Burger King used to have an ad campaign that proudly encouraged customers to have it their way: "Hold the pickles, hold the lettuce, special orders don't upset us." There are a lot of churches that are happy to allow their members to have it their way when it comes to doctrine. As long as you believe in Jesus and the resurrection, they really don't care what else you believe. I talked earlier in this book about a church I visited that had a "have it your way" view of baptism: do it, don't do it, dunk, or sprinkle—it didn't matter to them.

It's interesting to note that the apostles did *not* approach doctrine this way. Paul wrote to Timothy about the importance of correctly explaining the word of truth (2 Tim. 2:15). He also warned the church in Rome not to let people stir up division in the church by teaching doctrines that conflicted with the apostle's teaching (Rom. 16:17). And Peter warned about false teachers who would "cleverly" teach destructive heresies (2 Pet. 2:1). Those verses and many others are a mandate for modern church leaders to be on the lookout for teachings that don't line up with the Bible.

One of the ways false teachers create division in the church is by suggesting that *their* way of thinking and doing is more enlightened or more spiritual than everyone else's—implying (and sometimes more than implying) that if you don't agree with them, then your spirituality is lacking. You then have the false teacher and his posse feeling superior, the people who disagree with them feeling resentful, and quite a few people in the middle just feeling confused but choosing up sides according their friendships. That's a recipe for trouble if ever there was one, and the reason why church leaders must never look the other way when someone starts promoting a doctrine that doesn't square with Scripture.

Question #2: Is the Problem One That Keeps Coming Up?

A child getting an ear infection is common. A child getting an ear infection every few weeks is not common. About the third or fourth time it happens, Mom and Dad are going to call the pediatrician, the child is going to see the doctor and quite possibly be scheduled to have tubes put in his ears. When unpleasant things start happening on a regular basis, it's time to look more closely and see what can be done about it.

This is certainly true in church. I've seen countless kerfuffles that kicked up some dust but died out quickly and were one and done. In fact, I would put most church conflicts into this category. They're situation-driven, so when the situation is resolved, so too is the conflict. But some dust-ups are more personality-driven, which means that even if they're tamped down today, they could easily flare up tomorrow because the personalities are still there and likely unchanged.

One time, as the church I was serving was going through a situation that had some people upset, an elder asked me, "Mark, have you ever noticed that every single time we have a problem, so-and-so is right in the middle of it?" He was right. It didn't matter what the problem was about—one specific person always seemed to be involved. This is not good, of course, but at least it's a pretty clear indication of where the leaders ought to focus their attention if they want to clean things up.

Question #3: Does the Problem Involve Wolfish Behavior?

Pound for pound, wolves may well be the most fearsome animals on the planet. They are highly intelligent, coldly calculating, and drawn by the smell of blood. By some estimates, a wolf can smell a wounded animal from up to a mile away. Wolves have been known to lope alongside a large animal, such as a moose, leaping up and biting chunks out of its side and underbelly as it tries to run away.

It's significant that Jesus chose the wolf as a metaphor for those people who are extreme troublemakers among his followers (Matt. 7:15). Specifically, he says they are false prophets, but the wolf metaphor reveals that he's talking about more than just someone who is doctrinally confused. The wolf is a killer.

During my almost fifty years as a pastor, I encountered very few wolves, but when I did, it was scary. Such people often put on a show of spirituality as sheep's clothing for public consumption, but at heart they're ruthless. They will say or do just about anything, and they actually take personal satisfaction in damaging people. I'll never forget the time a man made an accusation against another man he didn't like. The accusation was that the man had inappropriately touched a high school girl, which would of course be a felony and result in jail time if it were true. The accused man vehemently denied the charge and challenged his accuser to produce a victim or witnesses, which the accuser couldn't do. But I don't believe the accuser ever intended to substantiate his claim. I'm convinced he just wanted to embarrass and shame someone he didn't like in order to damage that man's reputation. This is the kind of thing church wolves do.

Although there's no way to tell, I often wonder how many people there are who were driven out of the church and/or lost their faith because of the ruthlessness of a wolf within the body of Christ. I think the number would be staggering. Church leaders must be on the lookout for that person who whose behavior isn't just bad, but cold and ruthless. When one rears its ugly head, those leaders must act.

Question #4: Does the Problem Involve an Attack on Leadership?

The word for this is *insubordination*.

A number of years ago, one of the strangest problems I've ever seen came up. It had to do with the management of our church library. The library was open thirty minutes before and after every worship service so people could stop in and pick up or drop off books. During the service, the library was closed. Sounds simple, right?

Think again.

A handful of ladies started congregating in the library during the service. They closed the library all right (by closing the door), but then stayed in there and chatted while the rest of the congregation was worshiping in the auditorium. This was brought to the elders' attention by our nursery staff, serving down the hall. They said, "Why is there so much commotion and laughter coming out of the library while the worship service is going on? We thought the library was supposed to be closed."

The elders looked into the situation and informed the library ladies that they needed to worship in the auditorium during service times and not hang out in the library.

Problem solved, right?

Think again.

The next Sunday, the ladies were once again partying in the library as if nothing had happened. It was a clear case of insubordination. The elders decided to wait one week and give them another chance. The next week, the party in the library went on as usual, in complete defiance of the elders' instructions, prompting the elders to fire the librarian, confiscate all keys to the door, and establish a new plan involving new people.

Defiance of the church's leaders simply cannot be tolerated. The Bible commands Christians to submit to their elders and obey (Heb. 13:17), so the kind of behavior I just described, though it might seem mild in some ways, was sinful.

Think of it in terms of parenting. When you're at the supermarket and see a child who's completely out of control, the one thing you know for certain is that the child has been allowed to defy its parents at home without repercussions. Children do not suddenly become monsters when they enter a supermarket. They become monsters gradually, by repeatedly challenging authority and winning.

Church leaders are wise to take insubordination seriously.

Question #5: Does the Problem Carry the Whiff of Scandal?

Sin is sin, right? One is as bad as another, right? That's what we've all been told, and in a sense it's true. *Every* sin falls short of the glory of God (Rom. 3:23). But we're fooling ourselves if we think sins that carry the whiff of scandal aren't more damaging to the cause of Christ. They are indeed, for several reasons:

1. *News of a scandal spreads like wildfire.* This has always been true, but it's even more of a concern in the age of social media.
2. *News of a scandal morphs as it spreads.* It's like the game "Telephone," where a person whispers something into his neighbor's ear, and then that person whispers it to the next person, and so on, all the way down the line. When the last

person says aloud what was whispered in his ear, it barely resembles the original statement. Scandals are bad enough without embellishment and exaggeration, but even worse after they have traveled the grapevine.

3. *News of a scandal devastates and perhaps damages the faith of many.* It's called disillusionment—that feeling of being disappointed and brokenhearted and suddenly not knowing if you can trust anyone anymore.
4. *News of a scandal empowers the Lord's enemies.* Gleeful mocking and ridicule will be the order of the day. Every critic of the church will pull out and dust off his the-church-is-full-of-hypocrites speech and have a ball at the neighborhood coffee shop or around the water cooler at the office.

Church leaders simply must take any whiff of scandal seriously. Naturally, there's a limit to what can be done. We are not the FBI. We cannot tap phones and issue subpoenas. But when rumors of a potential scandal begin to swirl, at the very least, questions should be asked of the parties involved.

I want to close this chapter with a proverb that's made its way down through the centuries in various forms. Quoted in some form by multiple authors, going as far back as the thirteenth century, this little bit of wisdom offers a great reminder to leaders everywhere:

For want of a nail, the shoe was lost,
For want of a shoe, the horse was lost,
For want of a horse, the knight was lost,
For want of a knight, the battle was lost,
For want of a battle, the kingdom was lost,
So a kingdom was lost, all for the want of a nail.

When small problems are ignored, they often turn into big problems. Many a church has been severely damaged by turmoil that could have been avoided (or at least greatly minimized) if the elders had stepped in early on and addressed a relatively small problem. There are many leaders, even gifted ones, who hate confrontation and are inclined to avoid it if at all possible. There is sometimes a moment, however, when nothing short of confrontation will honor Christ and protect the church. It's a shame when we don't realize how critical that horseshoe nail was until the kingdom is on fire.

4

EXERCISE DISCIPLINE BIBLICALLY

No book about church troublemakers would be complete without an examination of what to do when one has to be dealt with. In a spiritually healthy church, this won't happen often. The positive culture will create a flow that pulls most potentially difficult situations in the direction of calm resolution. It's what happens when people who share a common love for Christ speak the truth to one another in love. I've actually overheard church members policing others by saying, "We don't act that way in this church." Or "You just need to deal with it and not cause a problem." Or "That behavior isn't very Christlike." It's similar to a healthy body being able to fight off infection, and it's beautiful.

Occasionally, however, a troublemaker will have to be dealt with. Let me just say, first of all, that this is a moment you must not run from or try to avoid. Too many leaders say, "Let's wait and see what happens. Maybe he'll think about it and fix the problem on his own." Or "Let's cut him some slack. He's been under a lot of stress lately." Or my personal favorite, "We shouldn't be too quick to judge. None of us is perfect either." I've heard all of these statements made in a clear effort to avoid or delay taking action. They're a sign of weak leadership that endangers the church by allowing the infection in the body to spread.

When troublemakers are doing their thing, the quicker you act, the less damage will be done. But also, the less pain there will be in the fix. Have you ever heard it said that the cure was worse than the sickness? This is usually only true when the sickness was ignored and subsequently required a fix that was far more catastrophic than it would have been if the problem had been dealt with early on. I have never once heard a church leader say, "I'm sure glad we waited until that problem got out of control before doing something."

But being *willing* to act is not enough. It's critical that you carefully follow the plan Jesus gave us in Matthew 18:15–17. There are other references to church discipline in the New Testament, but Jesus' words on the matter succinctly lay out the proper approach. There are six steps.

Step #1: Speak to the Offending Person Privately

Let's be honest. Most of the time, this is not what happens. It's much more common for people to tell everyone else about the person's offending behavior and never say a word to them. I doubt we even realize we're sinning when we do this. We think that because we have been sinned against, we're justified in proclaiming our pain to anyone who will listen. But Jesus is clear: The person who is hurt needs to speak to the one who did the hurting, which Jesus says should happen privately.

This conversation should also happen before too much time passes, but it must not happen until the offended party has had a chance to cool down. I've seen far too many instances where an offended person spoke to the one who caused the offense before the offended one had a chance to step back and process what had happened and pray about it. When that happens, the result is almost always bad. Either the wrong words are spoken, or there's too much heat in the tone of voice.

I'll also point out that this conversation should not come across as accusing or judging the other person. Rather, the offended person should communicate a desire to make things right. It's possible that the person at fault may not be aware of the hurt they caused. Or even if they are, then they might have been under pressure in ways the offended one didn't know about. People do have hard days and weak moments, which can result in atypical behavior. Paul's admonition in Ephesians 4:15 to speak the truth in love fits perfectly here.

Step #2: If the First Attempt Fails, Try Again—but This Time with Witnesses

The ideal situation would be to see peace made between the parties as a result of Step #1. If that doesn't happen, then others need to be brought into the situation, which means the matter is no longer private. One or two people should accompany the offended person back to the individual who caused the offense and revisit the issues involved. In selecting the person (or persons) who will participate in this second conversation, it would be wise (if possible) to choose someone who has a good relationship with the person who caused the offense.

Of course, there's always the possibility that the person being talked to might refuse to meet for a second conversation. I've seen situations where this was the case. I remember one instance where the person refused to answer the door after looking through the curtains and seeing who was on the doorstep. Another time, I accompanied someone to speak to a woman who happened to be in her backyard. Her husband let us into the house and went to tell his wife we were there. She went straight to her bedroom, slammed the door, turned the lock, and refused to come out. Her husband, who knew his wife had done something wrong and was supportive of our being there to talk to her, was unable to get her to come out. In a case like this, those wanting to work things out have done what they could and can have a clear conscience.

Ideally, this second step will produce repentance in the offending party, or at least a willingness to think and pray about what has happened. I've been in situations where even though things weren't completely resolved, progress was made and everyone left feeling better, if not great. In that case, you have something to build on. However, there's always the possibility the situation could deteriorate further. Anger might flare up. Even more hurtful words may be spoken. In that case, there is a next step.

Step #3: Inform the Elders

This is what is meant by "take your case to the church" in Matthew 18:17. No, Jesus doesn't specifically mention elders in this passage, but it makes sense to believe that's who he's talking about, given the shepherding role the Scriptures give to elders.

When the elders are informed about the situation, it should be done in private. The elders should ask questions to make sure they fully understand what happened. It's possible they might have their own concerns about how the offended party has handled things, and if so, they should express them. Or they might have some point of disagreement. Maybe they feel a sin was not committed, that the offended party overreacted, or that a minor offense occurred but was blown out of proportion. This is a situation where wisdom will be required.

Ultimately, they should take the information they have and act accordingly. If they feel a sin has been committed, that an innocent party has been wronged, and that needed repentance is not forthcoming, they need to move to the next step.

Step #4: Make a Third Visit

This one will be made by the elders. They will humbly and lovingly talk to the offending party. They will ask for that person's version of events. They may ask questions for clarification. If they still believe the person sinned, then they will talk about the need for repentance. If no repentance is forthcoming, then they will inform the person that they're going to proceed to the next step.

Step #5: Bring the Matter before the Church

Although there are no specific guidelines as to how this should be done, it's something that needs a lot of thought. What might be appropriate in one situation might not be in another.

For example, if the matter is well known in the community and is seen as a full-blown scandal, then full transparency would be advisable, meaning the matter might best be addressed at the conclusion of a Sunday worship service. On the other hand, if the matter is only known to a few people, then some kind of members-only meeting might be the best choice. As far as what is going to be said, the elders need to carefully craft them and then write them down. In such a sensitive situation, the last thing you want is for someone to say too much and reveal personal information people don't need to know. Equally problematic would be not saying enough, so that people leave the meeting confused. It would probably also be wise to send a letter to the church membership to inform those who were not at the meeting.

Only one time in my years as a pastor did we have to carry the discipline process this far. I remember feeling sick in my stomach as I walked to the pulpit to read the letter the elders had crafted. I read it slowly, trying to keep my voice even, trying not to break down. When I finished, I led the congregation in a prayer for the parties involved and closed the service. Afterward, a couple I had never seen before approached me and informed me that it was their first Sunday at our church. I immediately started apologizing for what they just witnessed, when they quickly interjected, "Oh, no! Please don't apologize! We wanted to tell you that we've never been so impressed in all our lives." They went on to tell me that they had attended a church for years that allowed troublemakers to run rampant over the entire congregation. The man said, "If the leaders of that church had done what you guys did today, maybe that church wouldn't have died." I was speechless and humbled. I have often wondered if God sent those two people to me at that moment as a kind of reminder that, as painful as it was, we did the right thing.

Step #6: Treat the Offending Person as an Outsider

It's important to think this one through. We live in a culture where it's common for people on opposite sides of any issue to harbor deep animosity. We've seen far too many instances of shouting and name-calling and even violence between people, for no reason other than that they disagree. This is not what Jesus is talking about when he says to "treat that person as a pagan or a corrupt tax collector."

Keep in mind that the whole purpose of church discipline is to bring repentance, to restore the troublemaker's relationship with God, their relationship with the person or people they hurt, and to bring peace to the body of Christ. This tells us everything we need to know about how to treat the troublemaker once they're placed outside our fellowship. You treat them the way you would treat any other sinner who needs Jesus. You don't shun them and give them the evil eye every time you see them. Instead, you say or do whatever you can to let them know that there's hope in the gospel, and that the door is open for them to return if they humble themselves and repent.

This is a point that must be carefully communicated to the entire congregation. Most people will never have seen a situation like this and may find it confusing: "We're kicking this guy out of our church, but we're still supposed to be nice to him?" Remember, there might be church members who work with the individual, or live next door, or bowl on the same team. This is quite likely in a small town, so people need to know that the person is not someone to hate but someone to love. Not someone to badmouth but someone to pray for. Not someone to criticize but someone to encourage.

Finally, the decision to remove the person from the fellowship needs to be communicated to the individual. Although face to face would be good, if things have reached this point, then it's unlikely the person would agree to yet another meeting. A letter may have to suffice. If so, then make it ring with humility and clearly state the elders' desire to see the person repent.

It's interesting to note that the words we've just considered in Matthew 18 were spoken by Jesus before the church even existed. He knew it was coming, of course, and was laying out some important instructions that would be a tremendous help later on. The disciples may have scratched their heads a bit when they first heard these words, but later you can be sure they were thankful for them. Years later, Paul would mention Hymenaeus and Alexander, two men he had "handed over to Satan" because of their blasphemy and the shipwreck of their souls (1 Tim. 1:20). Surely, Jesus' instructions helped shape this action.

I, too, am thankful for Jesus' clear instruction. On one particularly difficult occasion, it is not an exaggeration to say that the plan Jesus laid out, which we followed to a T, prevented what would have been a catastrophic upheaval in our church. I hope you never need to employ this plan. If you do, though, then do it to the letter. You'll be glad you did.

A PARTING NOTE

Thank you for joining me on this journey through one of the darker territories of church life. I want to be clear in saying that, for all the problems one can encounter in church, it is still among God's greatest gifts to us. I think of it like a house. Sometimes the roof leaks or the AC goes out or the toilet clogs, but what would you do without your house? There is no problem that would ever make me say, "That's it, I'm done. I'm going to go live in the woods." I love the church more than I can say, even with her imperfections, and I feel bad for those who choose to live in the woods because the house needs a few repairs.

I deeply appreciate the time you spent with this book. With so many great publications out there, I'm humbled you gave mine some of your precious time. I hope it helped. God willing, may we meet again in the pages of some future—and happier!—book.

Mark Atteberry
Central Florida

NOTES

1. Steven J. Lawson, *Faith under Fire: Standing Strong When Satan Attacks* (Wheaton, IL: Crossway, 1995), 201.

2. Guy Greenfield, *The Wounded Minister: Healing for Abused Clergy* (Grand Rapids: Baker, 2001), 17.

3. J. C. Ryle, *Holiness: Its Nature, Hindrances, Difficulties, and Roots* (Oregon City: Charles Nolan, 2001), 77.

4. Robert L. Short, *The Gospel according to Peanuts* (Louisville, KY: John Knox Press, 2000), 123–24.

5. Arthur H. Bell and Dayle M. Smith, *Difficult People at Work: How to Cope, How to Win* (New York: MJF Books, 2004), vi.

6. Art Markman, "Why Does the Past Seem Happy?," *Psychology Today*, December 18, 2012, https://www.psychologytoday.com.

7. "Carnegie Mellon Research Explores Nostalgic Preferences: Why the Past Seems Better," June 26, 2013, https://www.cmu.edu/news/stories/archives/2013.

8. Mark Atteberry, *The 10 Dumbest Things Christians Do* (Nashville: Nelson, 2006).

9. "Why Employee Satisfaction Matters to Shareholders," September 29, 2014, https://knowledge.wharton.upenn.edu/.

10. Lifeway, "The Power of Consistency," https://leadership.lifeway.com/2015/03/23/the-power-of-consistency-2/.

11. Marshall Shelley, *Well-Intentioned Dragons: Ministering to Problem People in the Church* (Carol Stream, IL: Word, 1985), 51.

12. Tom Hovestal, *Extreme Righteousness: Seeing Ourselves in the Pharisees* (Chicago: Moody Press, 1997), 81.

13. Larry Osborne, *Accidental Pharisees: Avoiding Pride, Exclusivity, and the Other Dangers of Overzealous Faith* (Grand Rapids: Zondervan, 2012), 142–43.

14. Dennis McCallum, *Satan and His Kingdom: What the Bible Says and How It Matters to You* (Bloomington, IN: Bethany House, 2009), 75.

15. "Why Church Leaders are Vulnerable to Infidelity and Pornography (& What to Do about It)," *Only You Forever*, https://www.onlyyouforever.com/why-church-leaders-are-vulnerable-to-infidelity-pornography/.

16. Jon Acuff, "Church Is the Best Place to Meet Dates," *Stuff Christians Like,* September 25, 2010, https://stuffchristianslike.net/2010/09/25/church-is-the-best-place-to-meet-dates/.

17. Leonard E. Reed, "I, Pencil: A Simple Instrument Teaches a Profound Lesson" Foundation for Economic Education, May 1, 1996, https://fee.org/resources/i-pencil/.

18. Patrick Goldstein, "Rotten Tomatoes Critics Agree: Jennifer Love Hewitt Is the Worst Actress of All Time," *Los Angeles Times*, June 7, 2011, https://www.latimes.com/entertainment.

19. Julia Carmel, "Jackie Stallone, Celebrity Astrologer and Sylvester's Mother, Dies at 98," *New York Times*, October 23, 2020, https://www.nytimes.com/2020/09/23/style/jackie-stallone-dead.html.

20. Mark D. Roberts, *Dare to Be True: Living in the Freedom of Complete Honesty* (Colorado Springs: Waterbrook Press, 2003), 179.

21. Timothy S. Laniak, *While Shepherds Watch Their Flocks: 40 Daily Reflections on Biblical Leadership* (Charlotte, NC: ShepherdLeader, 2007), 112.

22. John Maxwell, *The 21 Indispensable Qualities of a Leader: Becoming the Person Others Will Want to Follow* (Nashville: Nelson, 1999), xi.